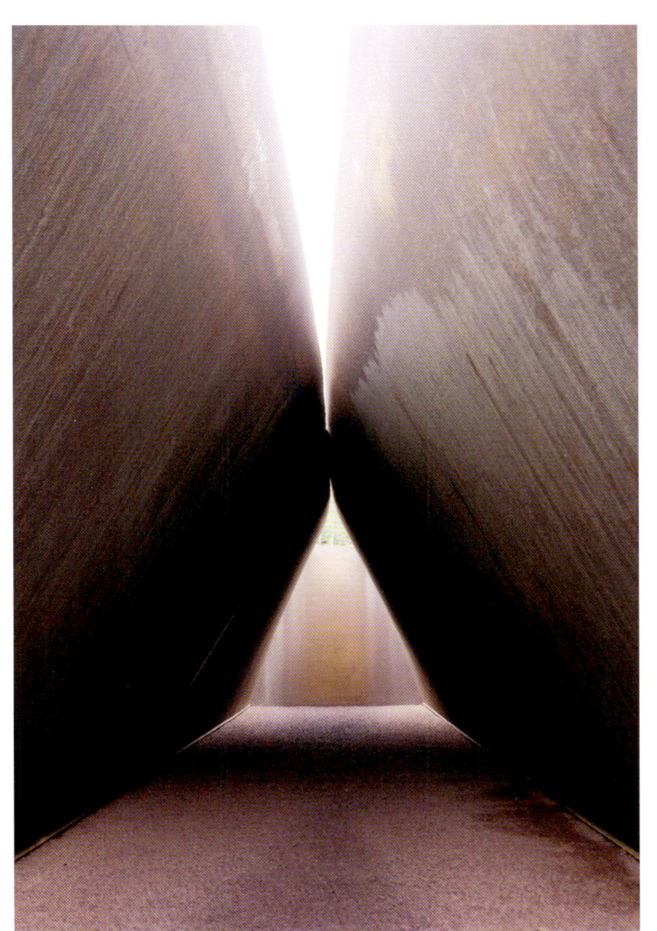

Michael Heizer

Glenstone

Contents

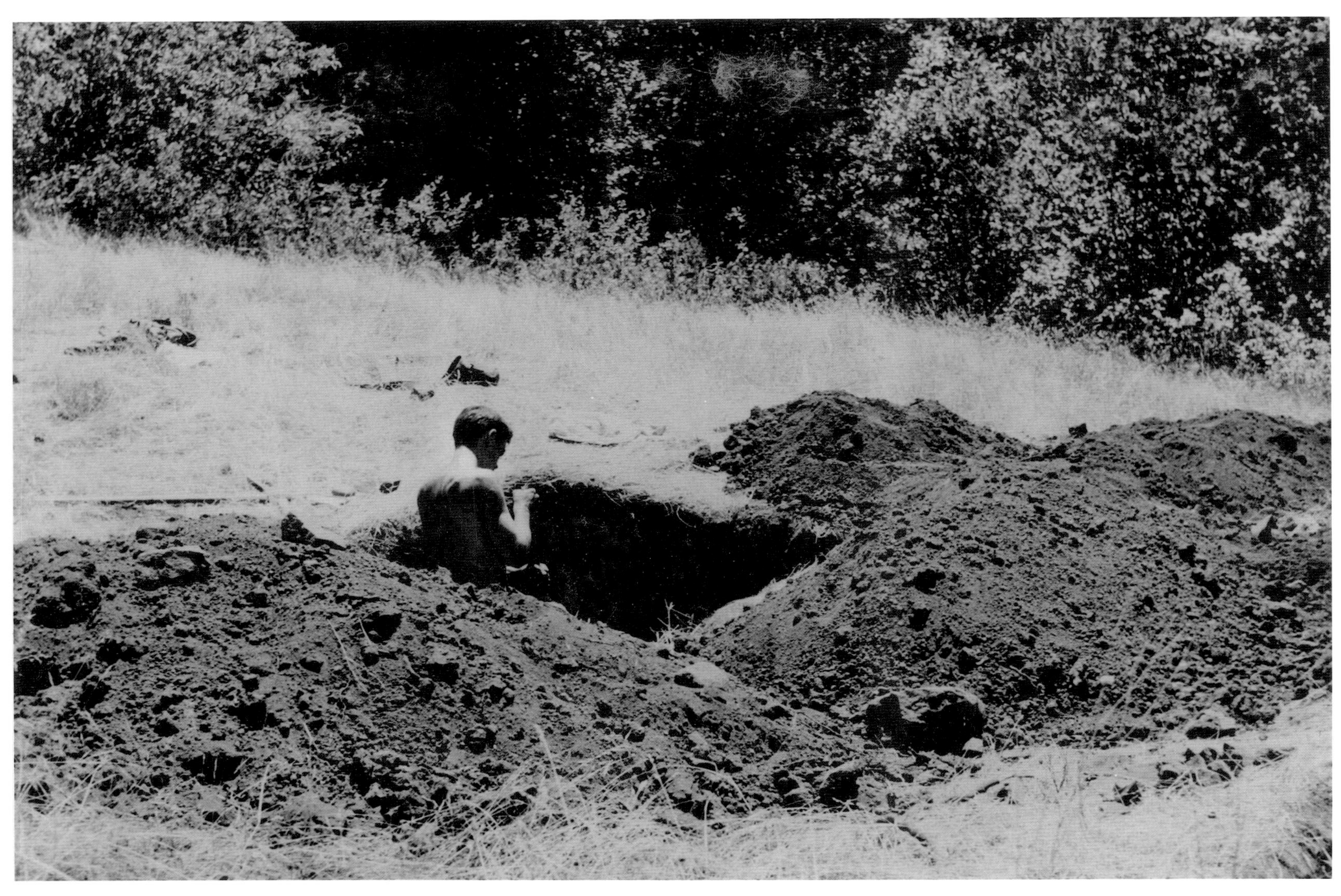

The artist pictured in the summer of 1961 on an environmental impact study near the future location of the Shasta Dam in Northern California. It was not uncommon to excavate obsidian glass artifacts unique to this geographical area.

Introduction

Emily Wei Rales

This publication commemorates the unveiling of two sculptures by Michael Heizer at the Pavilions at Glenstone: *Collapse*, 1967/2016, and *Compression Line*, 1968/2016. For the first time, multiple large-scale outdoor sculptures by the artist are now on permanent view in a museum setting. Heizer is best known for his massive sculptures that sprawl across expansive tracts of land in places like Garden Valley, Nevada; Bagnes, Switzerland; and downtown Los Angeles. For an artist who has spent a considerable part of his life making monumental statements in steel, concrete, and rock, it is perhaps not surprising that he prefers to let his work do most of the talking. In truth, Heizer's work needs little explication, because its power derives from facets of reality that dictate life on this planet: the laws of physics, the structural integrity of raw materials, and the vicissitudes of weather. While words may be applied to any of these phenomena, humans have had to contend with them since prehistoric times, long before the advent of language. Words are also ineffective when attempting to describe the intense, visceral reactions Heizer's work often provokes in viewers. Although we celebrate Heizer's achievement with this publication, we remind our readers that the texts and imagery in the pages that follow are but distant surrogates for his art, the full impact of which can only be experienced in person.

Heizer first built *Collapse* and *Compression Line* in the late 1960s on the dry bed of El Mirage Lake in the Mojave Desert in California. During this time, the artist was living in New York but made several trips west to construct what would later become the Mojave Projects, a group of fugitive sculptures, paintings, and drawings using materials from the earth applied directly on and in the ground. In the desert, the artist conceived *Compression Line* as a sixteen-foot-long, two-foot-wide, two-foot-deep triangular tunnel made of out of wood. On either side of the tunnel, he compacted native silt and fractured rock to generate a compressive force that bent the wood, causing the top edges in the midsection to meet. For the version he constructed at Glenstone, Heizer devised a structure made of weathering steel and increased the dimensions of the sculpture to seventy-five feet long, ten feet wide, and ten feet deep. Over two thousand cubic yards of soil were removed from the site to make space both for the sculpture and the massive earth-moving equipment required to backfill and compress that same volume of soil evenly around the sculpture, so that the steel plates would yield until they just touched in the middle. The imparted energy—the compression—as well as the resulting symmetrical catenary curves are integral to the work.

For the original *Collapse*, also built on a much smaller scale, Heizer placed wooden planks in a radial arrangement in a shallow rectangular pit. For Glenstone's iteration, Heizer again chose weathering steel as the material for what he calls the "negative earth liner," or the below-ground box inside which fifteen steel beams of varying lengths were placed with the aid of a construction crane. Heizer's seemingly random, "chaotic" positioning of the beams creates a dynamic, angular composition of negative spaces, implying that chance and gravity, rather than formal considerations, were responsible for their arrangement. Much larger now than when initially conceived, the box measures twenty-four feet by thirty-six feet by sixteen feet deep, while the beams range from sixteen to forty-two feet in length. Two of the longest beams stack one on top of the other, reaching a height of almost six feet above grade. Intensifying the experience further is the diagonal orientation of the work within a rectangular enclosure that is open to the elements—the only space of its kind in the Pavilions.

When discussing his sculpture practice, Heizer insists that he is primarily concerned with the physical limits of materials rather than their aesthetic qualities.[1] Indeed, the shape of *Compression Line* is determined by the deformation properties of the steel plates as well as the compaction properties of the soil. Yet to say that Heizer is only interested in material affordances would be to oversimplify his art. After all, human will and ingenuity remain crucial to revealing these physical characteristics. Over the course of the installation, Heizer and his associate Kody Rudder operated two twenty-six-ton wheel loaders, powerful machines typically used in agricultural and construction projects. With expert precision, the men drove the giant earth-moving vehicles parallel to the sculpture, pushing both the soil and the steel to their maximum potential. Even at the grandest scale, Heizer exhibits a highly refined aesthetic sensibility and exacting attention to detail. This dialectic between physical reality and aesthetic criteria has long been a mainstay in Heizer's work. His account of the construction of *Double Negative*, 1969–1970, the seminal earthwork consisting of two enormous cuts in a wall of rock in the Mormon Mesa in Nevada, clearly illustrates this symbiosis:

> As the volume of material grew, the length of the cut became greater and the base longer. Ultimately, the decisive factor in recognizing the completion of the work depended on the volume and shape of the two spills or spoils. . . . The cuts were kept active, to produce material, until the gravity-formed volumes appeared to become balanced and related visually. In other words, the cuts in the mesa became material sources for the spills. Even though the spills look random, they were carefully developed through continuous cutting and pushing, until they assumed sculptural presence.[2]

Heizer brings a similar formal rigor and fine touch to the design, intent, and construction of *Compression Line* and *Collapse*. In describing the meeting of the two steel plates in *Compression Line*, Heizer says they "just kiss" in the middle. Likewise, the beams in *Collapse* are unlike anything one might find on a building construction site. Massive in size but gentle in profile, the beams feature subtly rounded edges, making the points of contact between them appear less abrasive than elegant.

The facts and figures cited above begin to give a sense of the monumentality of Heizer's sculptures, especially in relation to the architecture that surrounds them. References to architecture have been of interest to Heizer since he built *Double Negative*, whose voids, he later discovered, could contain the Empire State Building lying on its side. Whereas *Double Negative* is sculpture that creates its own architecture, Heizer's works at Glenstone engage the existing architecture of the museum in what might be described as a tense yet respectful confrontation. These works are not site-specific in the traditional sense, whereby art is conceived with the parameters of a particular context in mind. To the contrary: *Compression Line* slashes through the earth just outside the museum's perimeter, not far from the underground drainage systems necessary for waterproofing the building, while *Collapse* is barely contained within the four walls of the roofless room designed to house it. These sculptures, Heizer seems to say, need no shelter. They may be enclosed and adjacent to architecture, but by no means are they tamed by it. As writer Paula Deitz observes, his works "reinforce the surrounding architecture by their use of basic forms and methods of construction—historical states, as it were, of architecture itself. Yet they are also a reminder of the wilderness that civilization sometimes thinks it has permanently replaced."[3] The disappearance of wilderness at the hands of civilization is a frequent lament of Heizer's, though he also believes that nature and culture can coexist under the right circumstances.[4] For *Compression Line*, he rejected an initial proposal to pour a solid concrete foundation to support the sculpture, and instead designed an open rectangular footing that allows water to pass through the void and drain directly into the ground as the natural water cycle would dictate. In these uncertain times, when environmental despoliation continues unabated, Heizer believes that respect for Mother Earth is paramount, a philosophy to which Glenstone also passionately subscribes.

It has been an honor and a pleasure to work with Michael Heizer on the conception and execution of these sculptures. We thank him for his enthusiasm, persistence, and most of all, his generosity in giving Glenstone his art, his time, and his words for this publication. We would like to acknowledge Mary Heizer and Wendy Rudder of the Triple Aught Foundation, both of whom were instrumental in managing administrative details from afar. We are grateful to Heizer's close associates Kody Rudder and Curt Weihz, who assisted the artist during numerous phases of planning and construction. From Budco Enterprises, we recognize Joe Vilardi, Ray LaChapelle, John Barbieri, Joe Berlese, and Ed Di Dinato, who worked seamlessly with the artist's team and the museum staff to assemble *Collapse* and complete finishing touches on *Compression Line*. From KC Fabrications we thank Chris Powers and Kurt Wulfmeyer. For engineering analysis and oversight, we are indebted to Ron Elad and Philip Skellorn of BuroHappold as well as Dmitri Jajich of Skidwell, Owings & Merrill. Aquatic Resource Restoration Company, led by R. Lee Irwin, performed an excellent job of grading and backfilling around *Compression Line*. We thank him and his associates Eric Deller, Stephen Walker, and Josh Guinn, as well as soil consultant Bill Khouri of Schnabel Engineering DC, and site surveyor Don Mitchell of VIKA. Thanks are also due to Michael Trudeau, project architect with Thomas Phifer and Partners. We are grateful to Kara Vander Weg of Gagosian Gallery for her assistance in coordinating a myriad of details along the way.

I would like to applaud my extraordinary associates at Glenstone, who collaborated on all aspects of bringing this project to fruition. Nora Severson Cafritz, Stephen Carrick, and Valentina Nahon worked tirelessly alongside a larger team that included Karina Barrera, Rick Boger, Jose Garcia, Martin Lotz, Eric Love, Mark Matovich, Steven O'Banion, Matthew Partain, and Charlotte Reineck. For the stunning images on these pages, we are grateful to photographers Jerry Thompson and Paul Tukey, who captured the sculptures at various stages of construction. In addition, we thank Ali Nemerov and Fanna Gebreyesus, designers Joseph Logan, Rachel Hudson, and Katy Nelson, printer Danny Frank, and editor Claire Lehmann for their contributions to this publication.

NOTES

1. "The thesis of those works was phenomenological, actual physical limits, not aesthetics. I had been painting and those were aesthetics. Sculptural meant there was potential for physical limits. These works were not aesthetic; they were real." Michael Heizer, in conversation with Emily Wei Rales, 2014.
2. Julia Brown, "Interview," in *Michael Heizer, Sculpture in Reverse*, ed. Brown, exh. cat. (Los Angeles: Museum of Contemporary Art, 1984), 24.
3. Paula Deitz, "Downtown in the Desert," in *Michael Heizer*, 76.
4. Michael Heizer, conversation.

Collapse, 1967/2016

Collapse, 1967/2016, is a steel sculpture comprised of fifteen massive beams arranged in a cavernous, topless box sunk into the earth. The beams range from sixteen to forty-two feet in length, and their placement appears both haphazard and delicate, setting the innate weight of the material and the gentle interplay between the various beams in opposition. Commissioned for Glenstone, *Collapse* is based on a wooden model originally created in 1967, which embodies the artist's study of chaos structure. At Glenstone, the work is installed in an open-air structure designed in collaboration with the artist.

A588 steel, 36 × 24 × 16 feet (1097 × 732 × 488 cm)

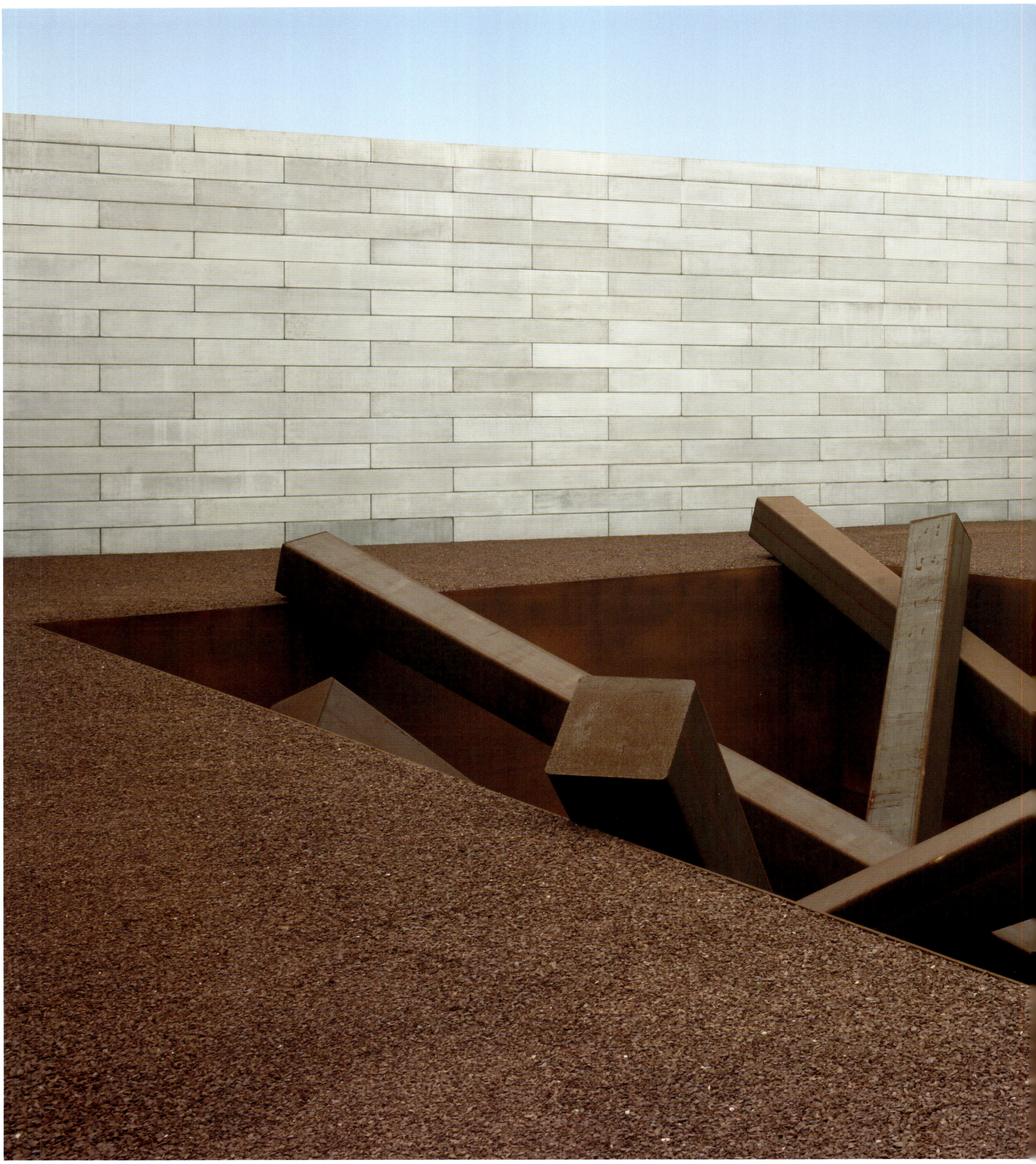

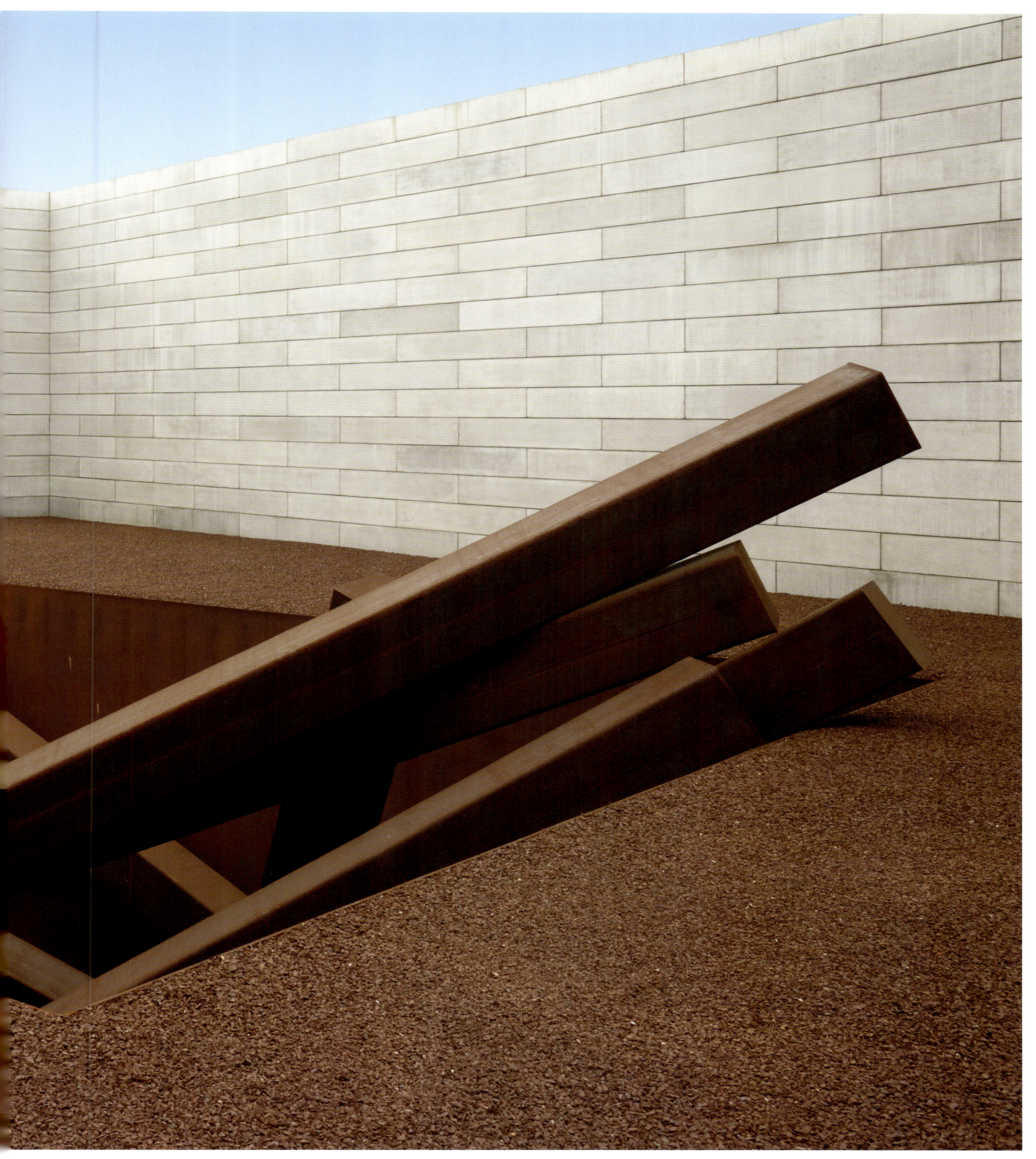

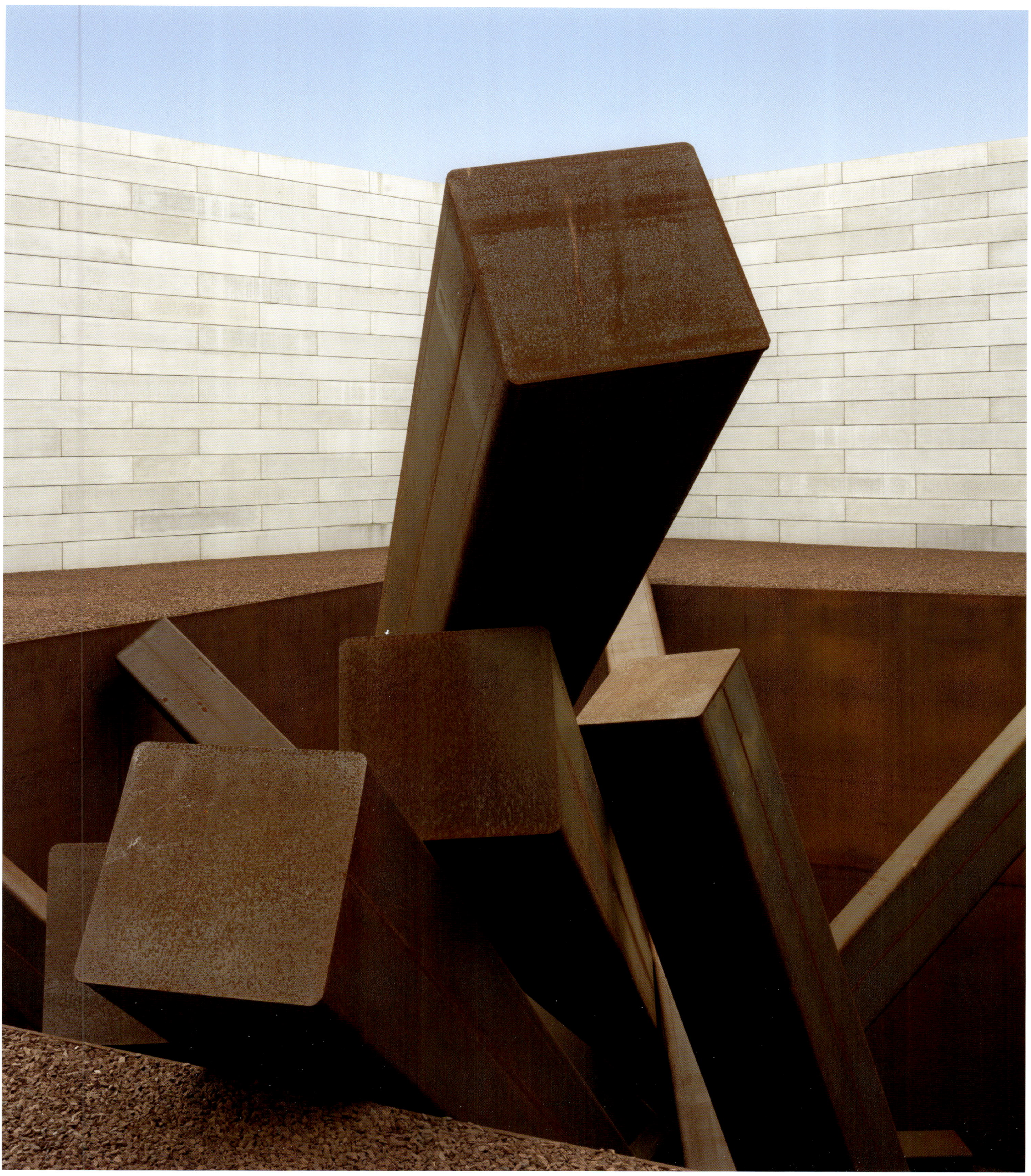

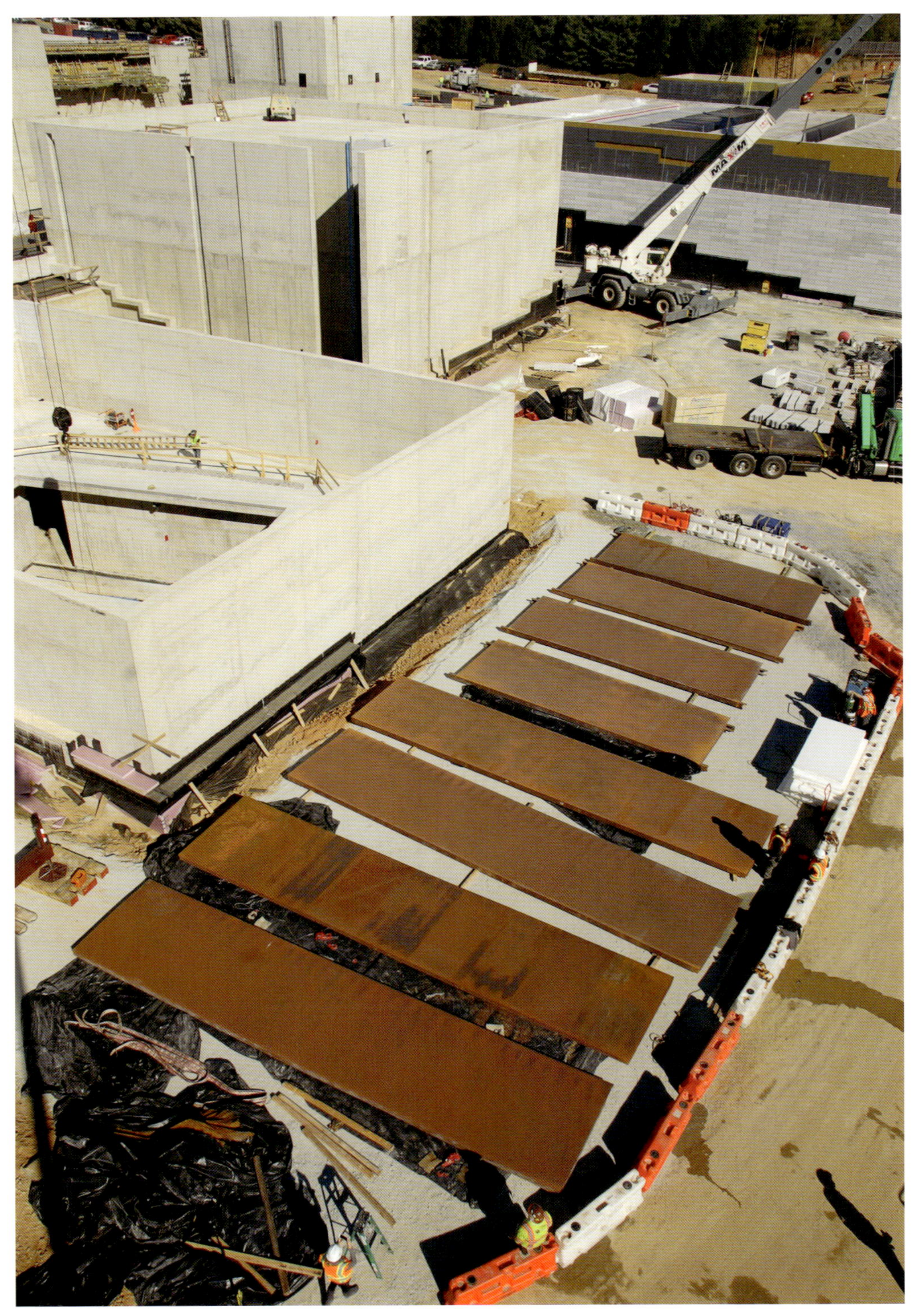

A bird's-eye view of the eight steel panels that comprise the walls of the rectangular box that houses the beams of *Collapse*, awaiting installation at Glenstone in October 2015. Over the course of several days, each panel was individually rigged over the purpose-built walls while the building was still under construction.

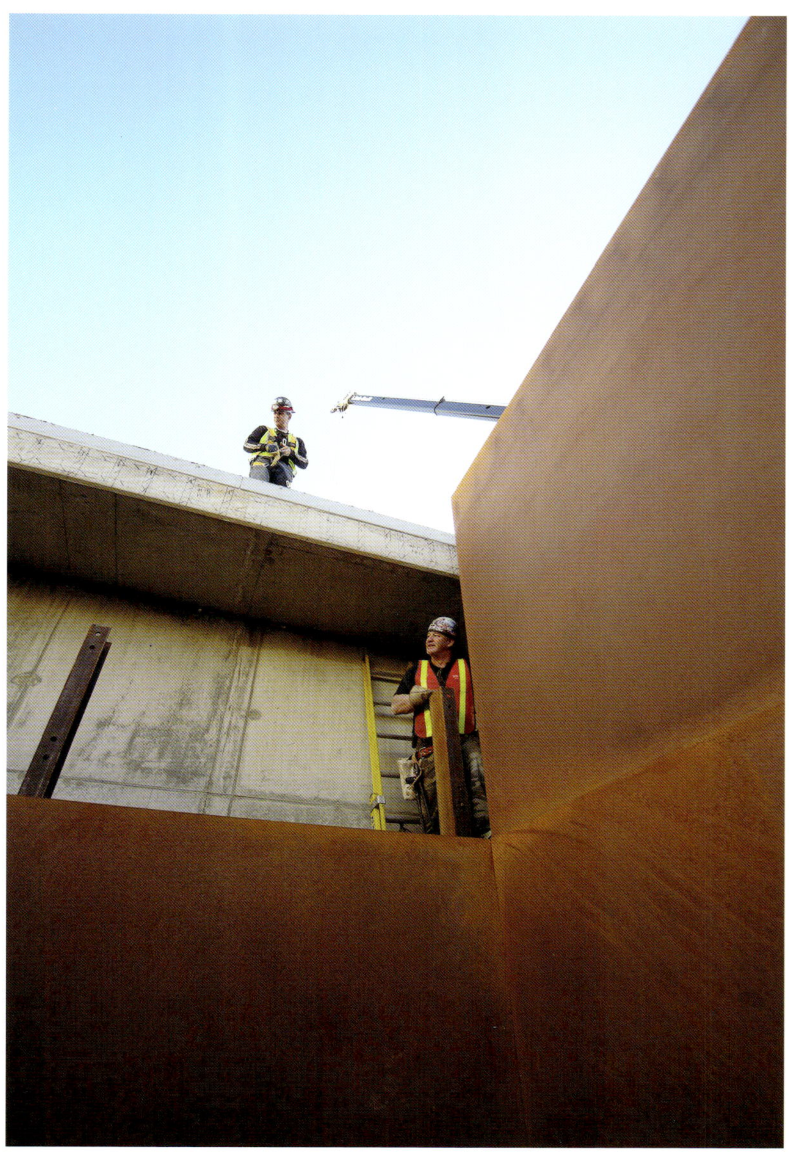

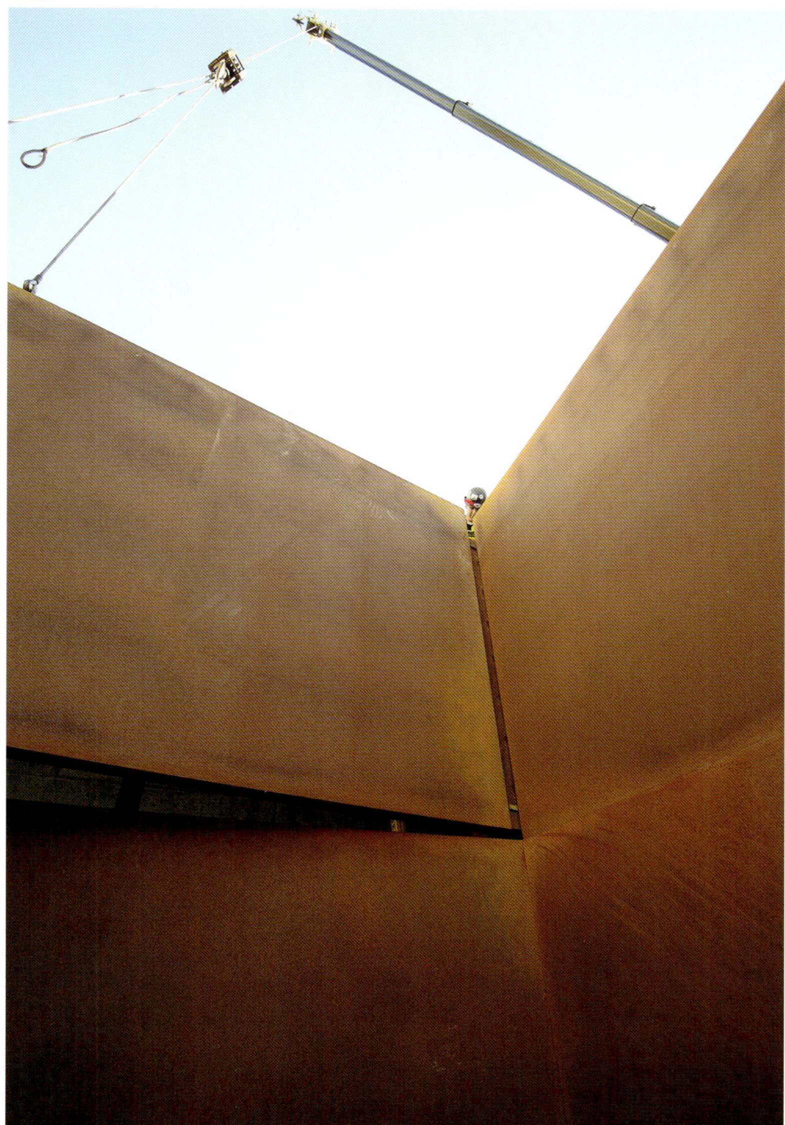

The northwest corner of the interior of *Collapse*'s subterranean box is jointed together.

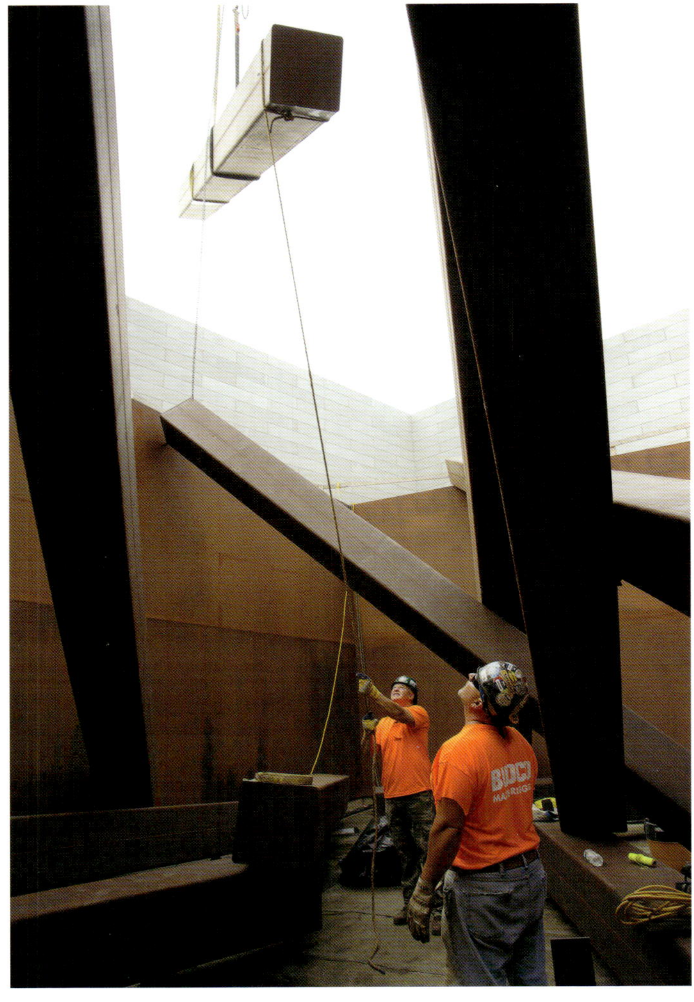

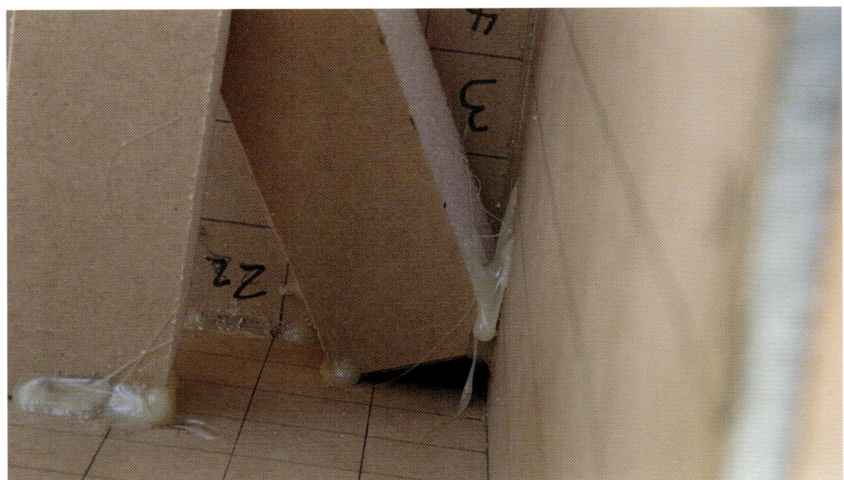

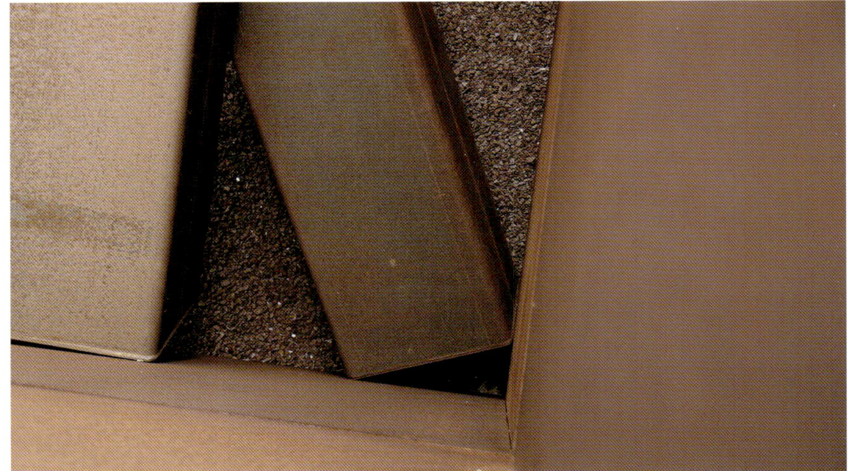

Left: Riggers supervise the precise positioning of beams inside the walls of *Collapse* during installation at Glenstone, July 2016.

Top: Detail of the scale architectural model of *Collapse*, rendered from the original wood maquette created by the artist in 1967.

Bottom: Detail of the corresponding steel beam in its final placement in summer 2016.

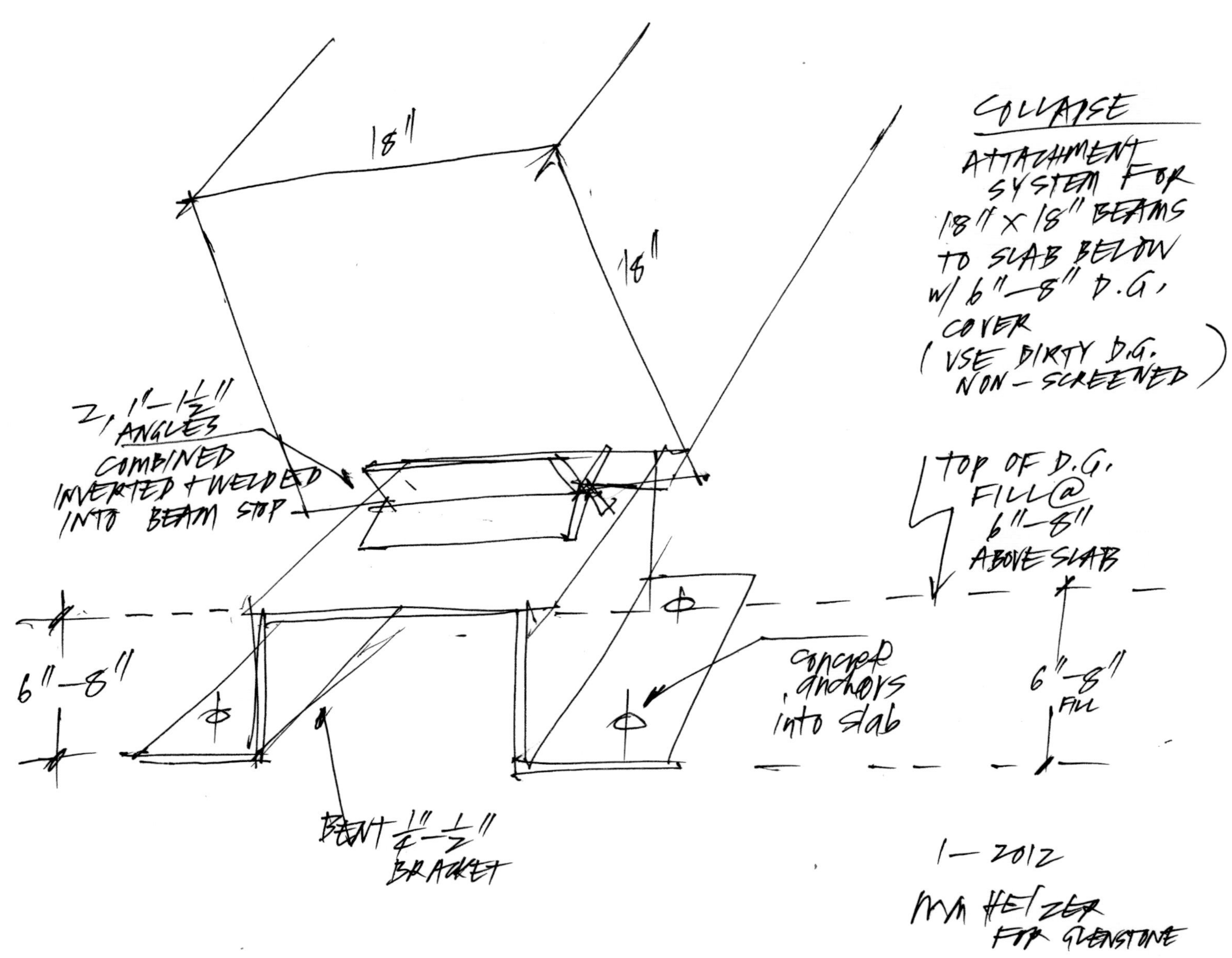

Artist's sketch of the bracketing strategy used to attach the steel beams to the concrete slab at the bottom of the sculpture. In the end, the artist decided that argillite, an angular crushed rock, was the right material to cover these brackets and the slab to which they are attached.

Compression Line, 1968/2016

Compression Line, 1968/2016, is a monumental concave steel sculpture embedded into the landscape. *Compression Line* is surrounded by twenty-two hundred cubic yards of compacted soil, the resulting pressure of which causes the two sides of the sculpture to compress inward and meet at the midpoint. Commissioned for Glenstone and installed by the artist, the work derives from an earlier version. *Compression Line* embodies the artist's interest in isolating and presenting physical phenomena as content for sculpture, as well as the formal complexities of negative space.

A588 steel, 75 × 10 × 9½ feet (2286 x 305 x 288 cm)

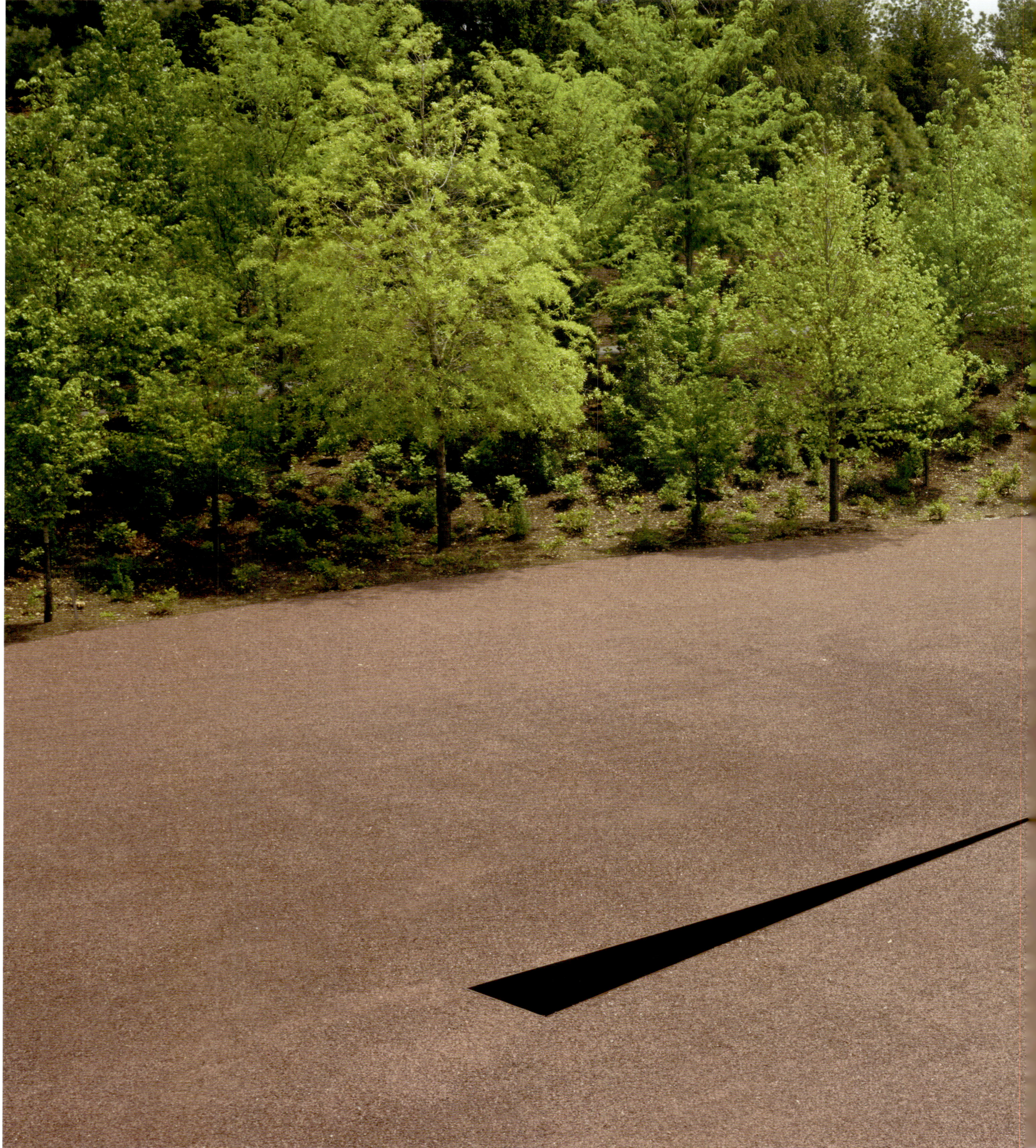

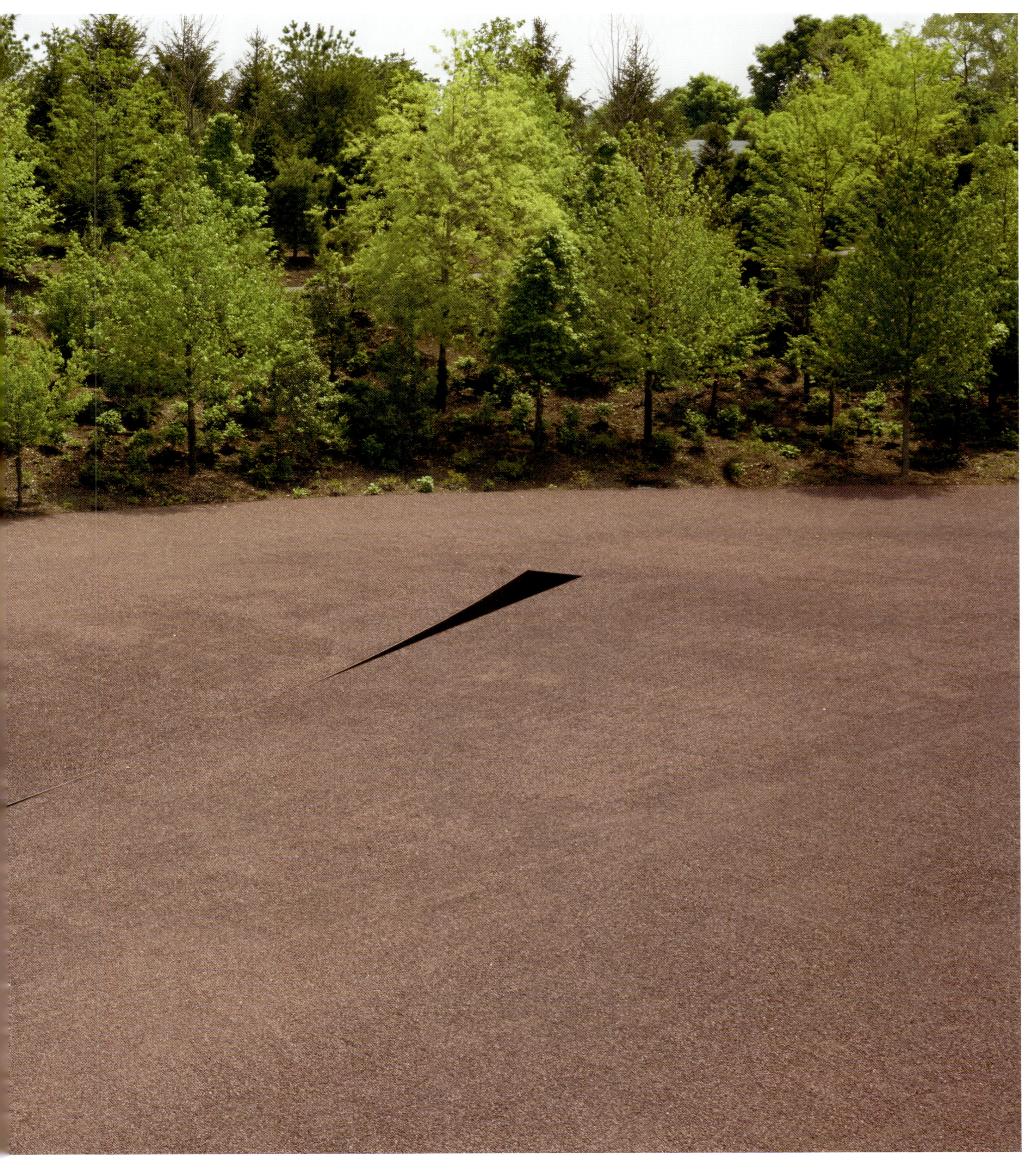

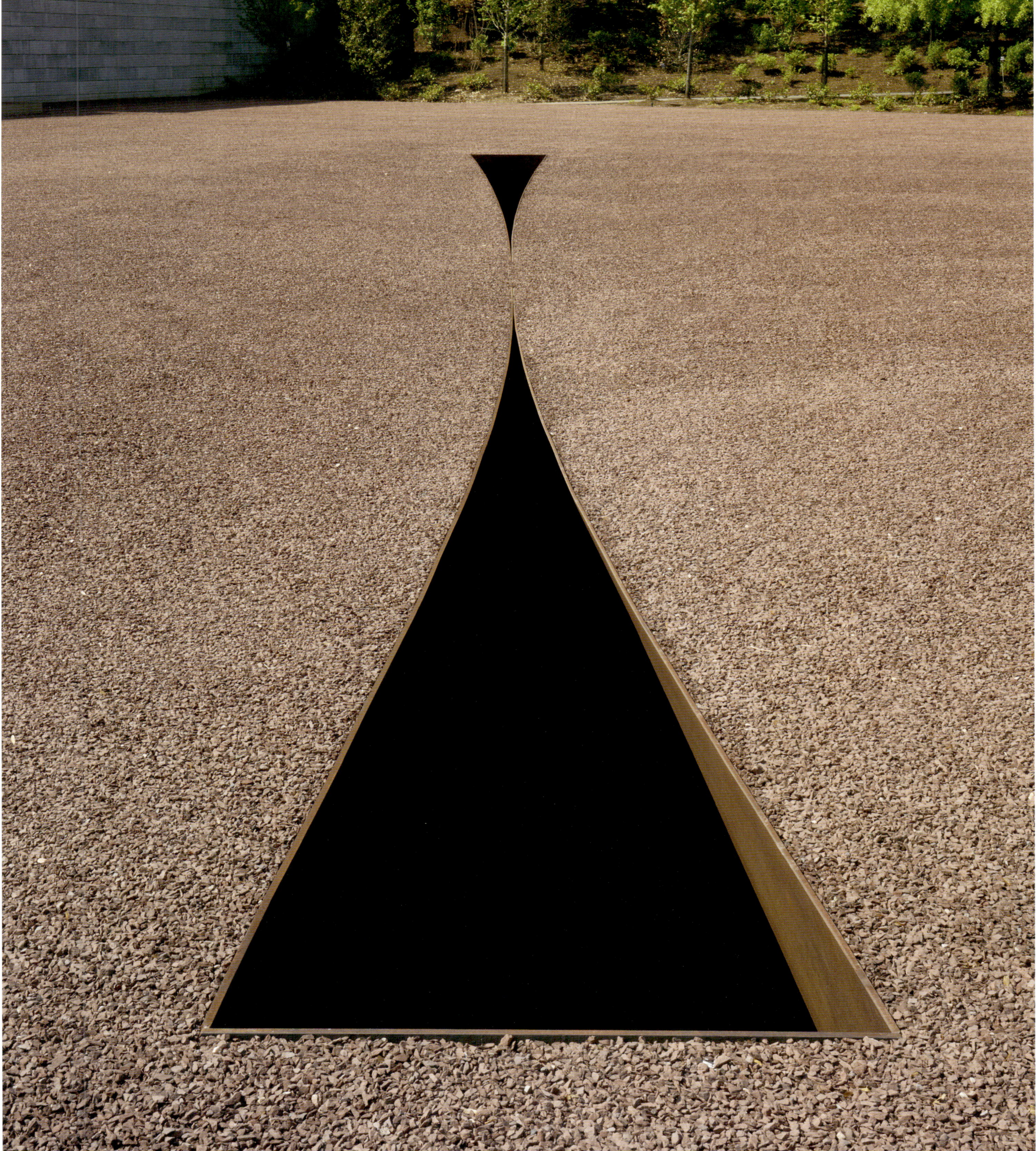

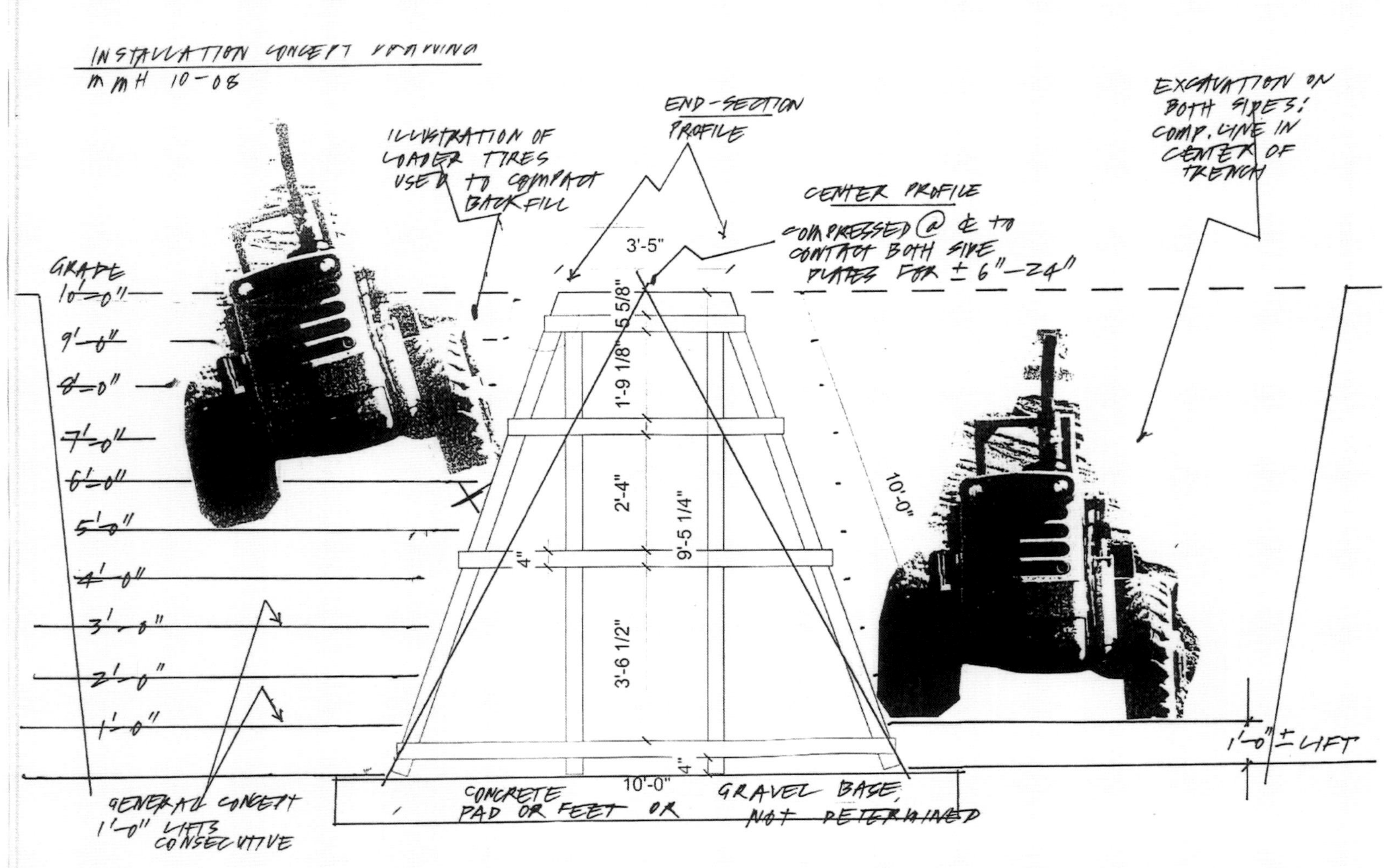

The artist's 2008 concept sketch for the installation of Glenstone's *Compression Line*, illustrating the simultaneous use of two Caterpillar 966K wheel loaders backfilling the engineered soil up to the weathering steel's top edge.

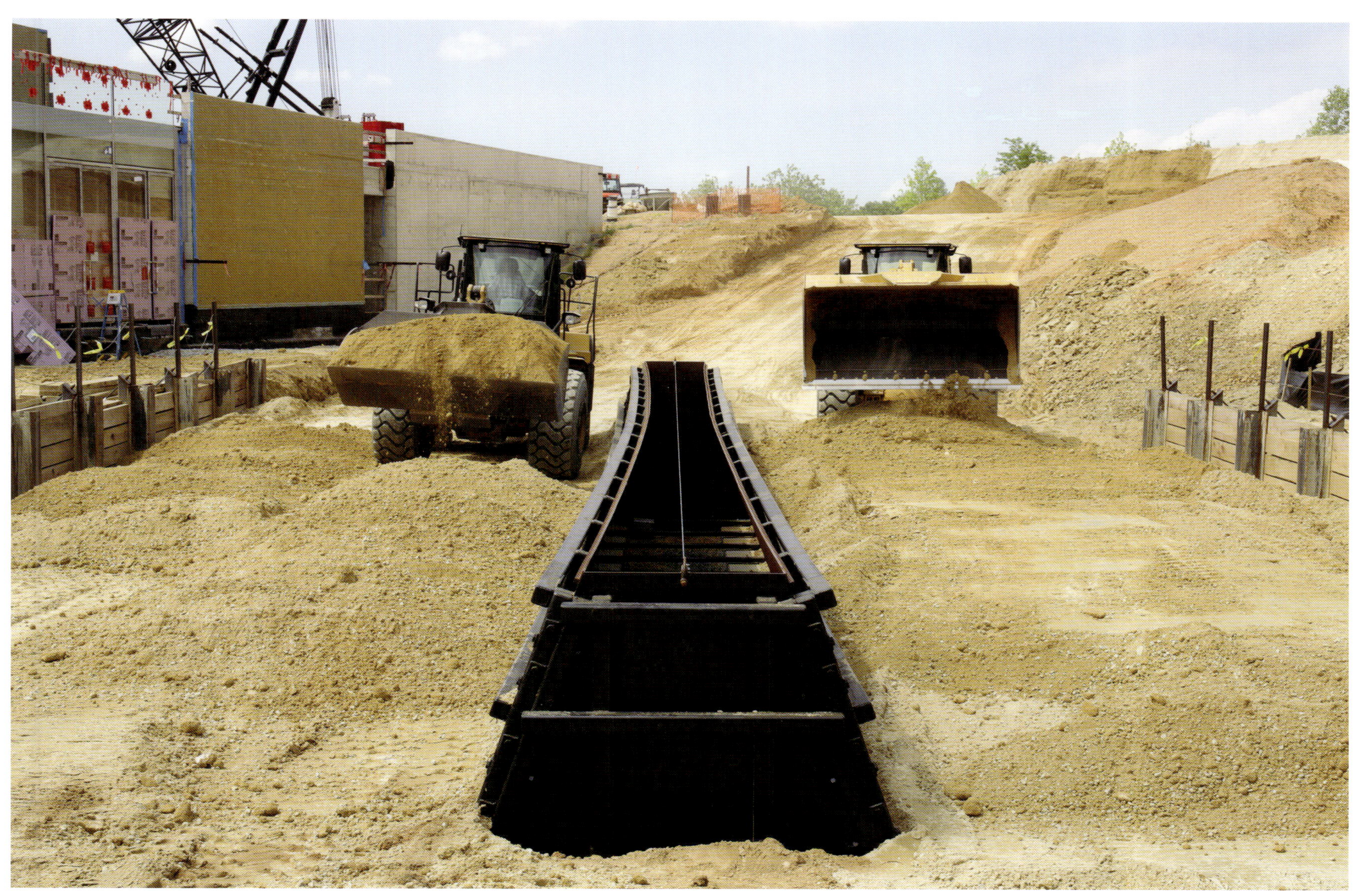

The artist (left) and assistant Kody Rudder (right) simultaneously backfilling engineered soil along the two sides of *Compression Line* in summer 2016. At this stage, the sides are beginning to bend toward each other at the midpoint from the pressure of the backfilled soil.

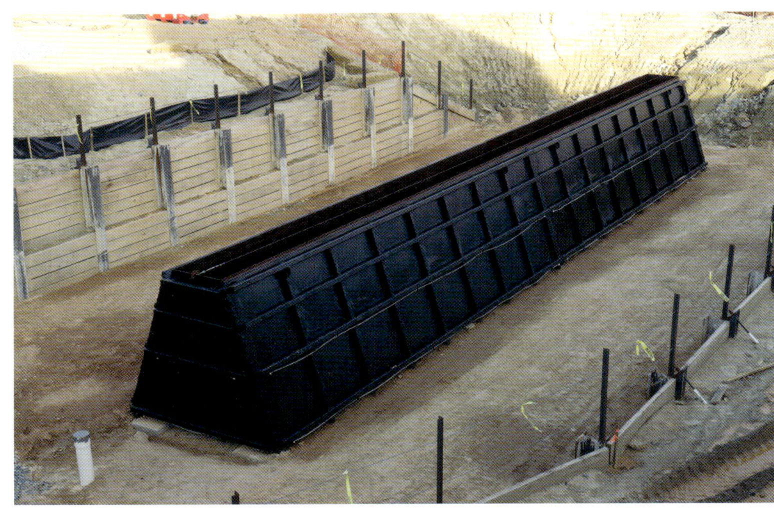

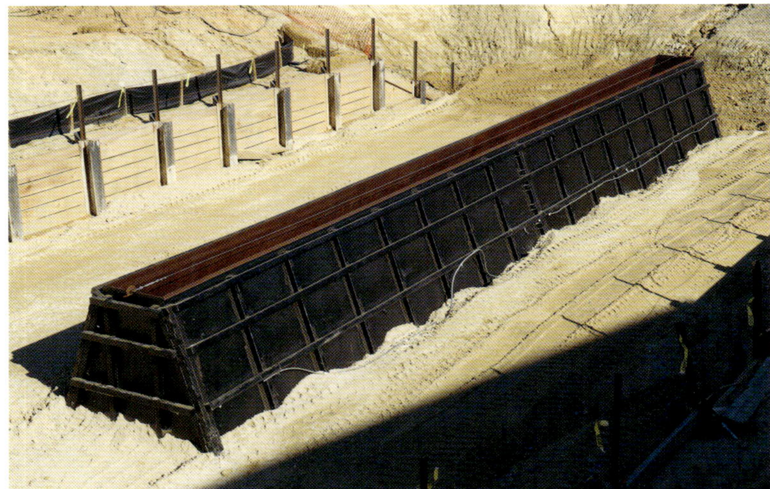

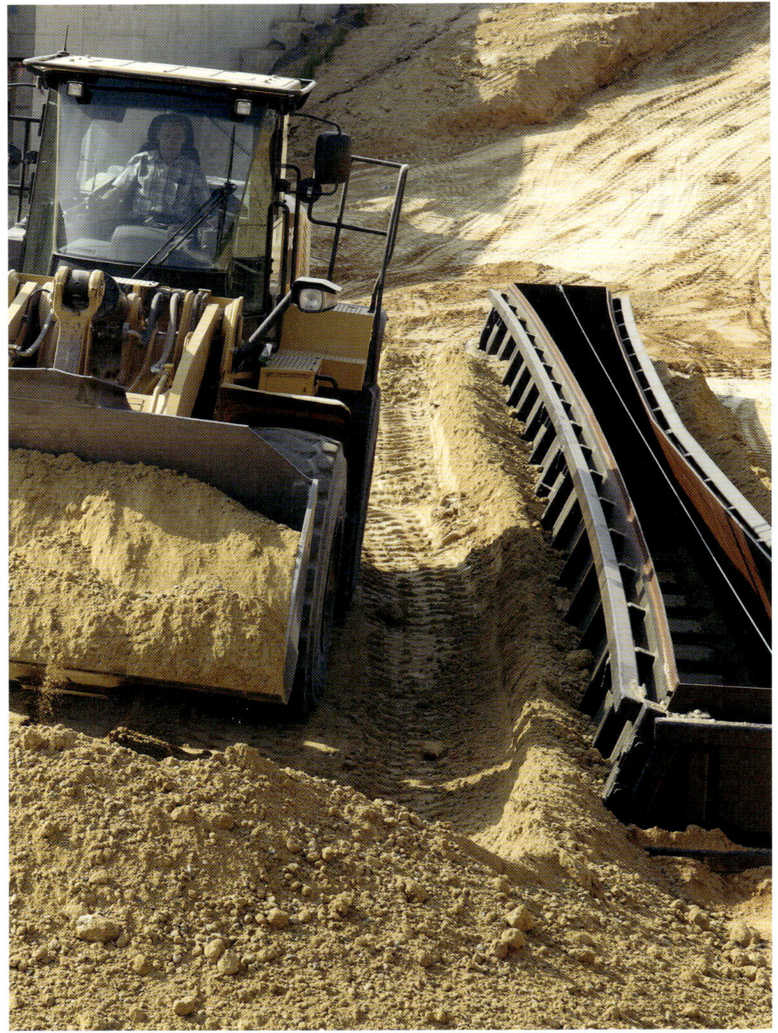

In full, it took three days to move and compress twenty-two hundred cubic yards of engineered soil against the sculpture. The various levels of compaction are illustrated above.

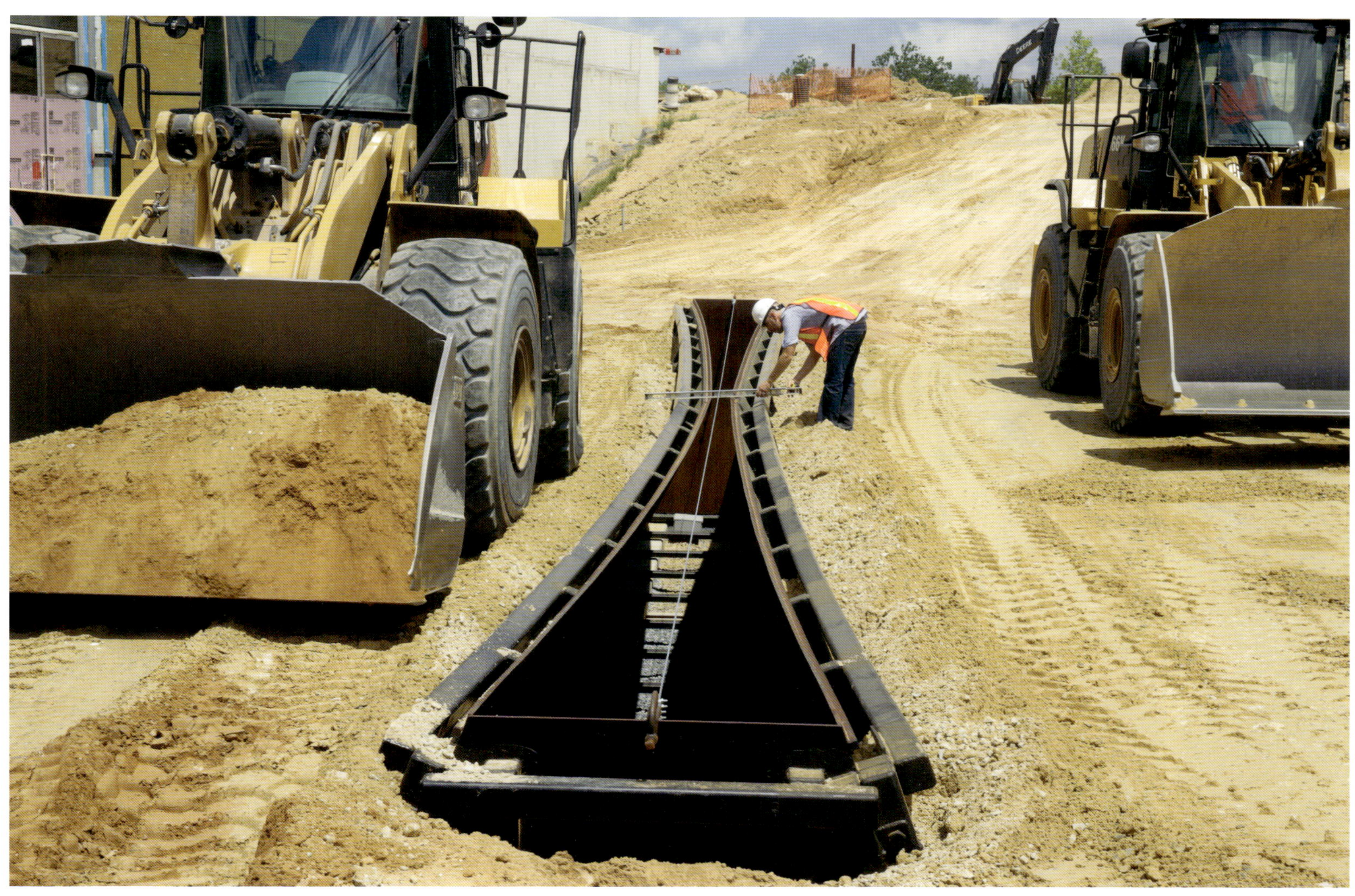

Structural engineers check the artist's progress as the sculpture approaches the moment when the soil's pressure will cause the two weathering-steel panels to touch at the midpoint.

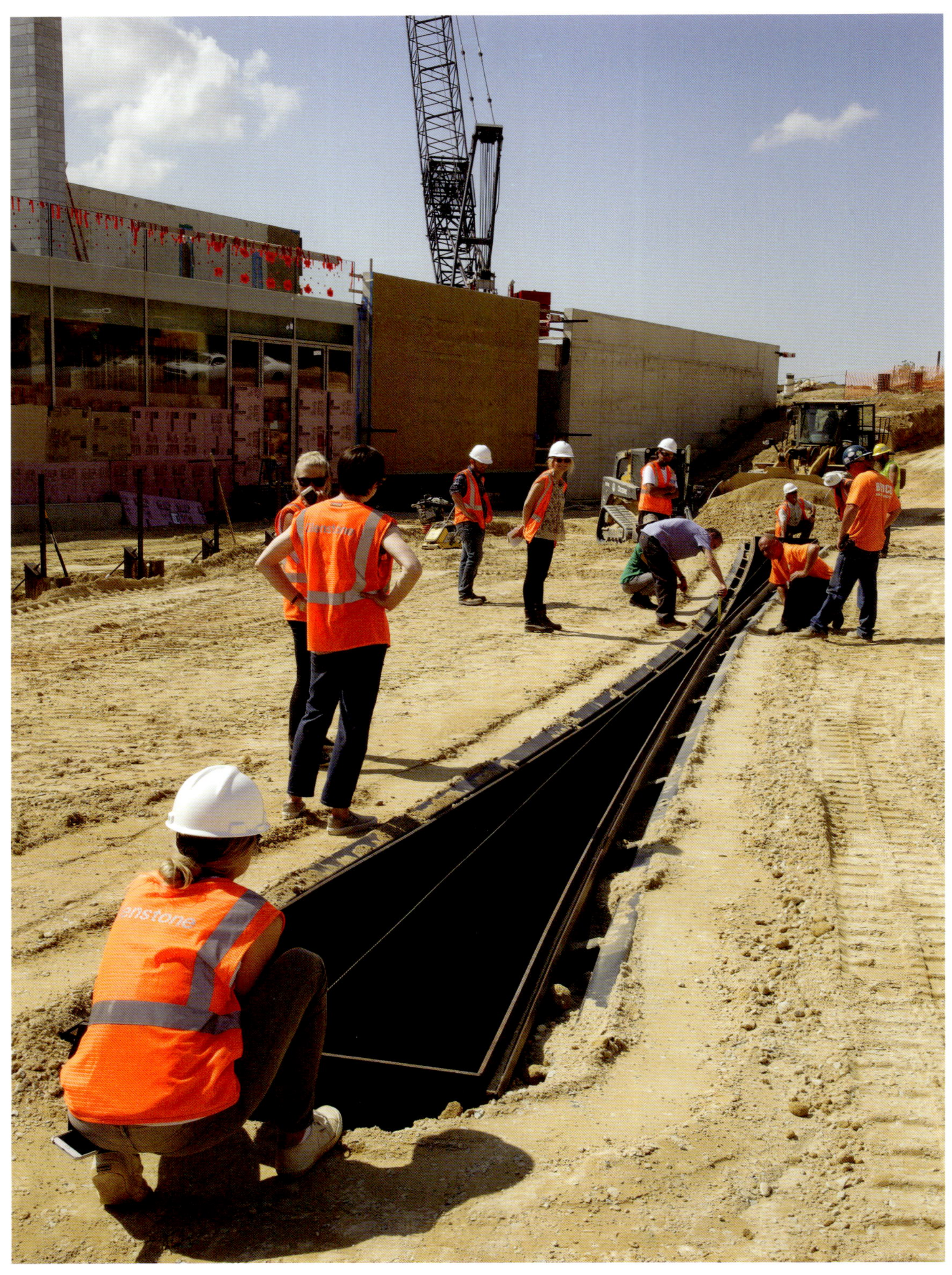

The artist inspecting the point at which the two sides touch.

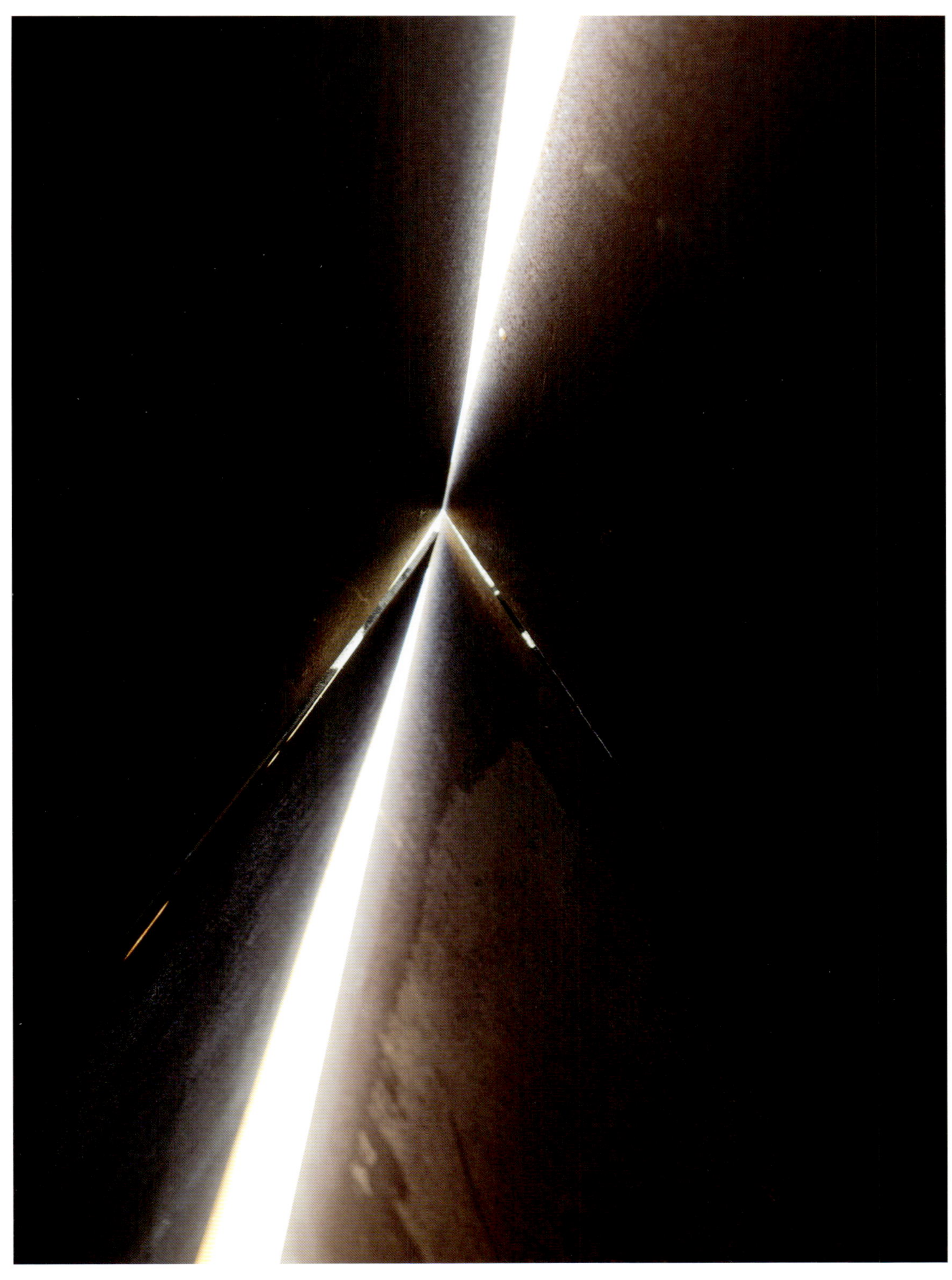

The interior of *Compression Line*, shown from below after compression was achieved.

Interview with Michael Heizer

Emily Wei Rales

Garden Valley, Nevada, March 20, 2014, 2:36 p.m.

EMILY WEI RALES: I understand *Compression Line* and *Collapse* originated around the time of the Nine Nevada Depressions. How did you first conceive of the sculptures, how did you select the original sites, and how did you conceive of the forms? How did they relate to the Nine Nevada Depressions?

MICHAEL HEIZER: *Compression Line* is before the Nine Nevada Depressions. Both are from 1968. The first *Collapse* I made in the Mojave is very different from the *Collapse* I developed in New York in 1967, and a later version from Nevada.

I installed the *Compression Line* on Mirage Dry Lake the morning after Bobby Kennedy was assassinated in Los Angeles. While we were digging the hole in the ground, the truck radio was on and we were hearing the thing all morning. I have always carried that association with the *Compression Line*. The year Bobby Kennedy died is how I remember the date. The content of the works is structural deformation.

EWR: Did you have a very clear idea of what the sculpture was going to look like before you actually built it? Were you aware of how the wood would respond, or was it just an exploration?

MH: I built things as a kid and worked as a carpenter. I dug holes in the ground and filled them in. It worked the way I thought it would. It compressed evenly, even the curvature. It is under pressure, in tension.

EWR: Do you recall how you came up with the aesthetic idea to do that initially?

MH: The thesis of those works was phenomenological, about actual physical limits, not aesthetics. When I had been painting, that was aesthetics. Sculpture meant there was potential for physical limits. These works were not aesthetic: they were real. That's where my mind was.

EWR: That was a period of tremendous activity for you.

MH: Most people in their early years are active. I had nothing to lose, Vietnam was happening, and the world was coming to an end. It was radicalized. Everything happened then. It was a huge transition in culture and thinking. That's how I remember it and think of it today.

EWR: When did you first realize you wanted to be an artist?

MH: I always was, ever since I was born. I never thought anything else.

EWR: What about Nevada—what is it about this place that led to forming those works?

MH: My father's father came to Nevada in the late 1800s. He got a degree in mining engineering in Reno. My other grandfather—my mother's father—was a petroleum geologist and later was with the Division of Mines of California. I spent time with them when I was young. My father was raised in Nevada and some of my family is still in Nevada. It's not like I showed up here as an exotic place to build artworks. I have spent a lot of time here since I was a kid.

EWR: But early on you were in San Francisco. How did you find your way to New York?

MH: I was in San Francisco for a year or so and got a studio there. There was a sculptor upstairs named Chuck Ross, and we became friends. He was moving to New York and told me about what was going on there. I met another sculptor, Bob Hudson. I got the picture from both of them that New York was the place, so I left. I think I was twenty-one or twenty-two when I went to New York. I drove there with another artist who had been at the San Francisco Art Institute and another guy. We went there in 1966.

EWR: But you weren't there very long.

MH: I never left. I maintained a studio there since '66. It was only fifteen years ago that I closed my studio on Greenwich Street, which I didn't use anymore because I couldn't travel. I always had studios in New York and just put locks on them when I was gone. My first studio was on Mercer Street and I kept it until 1970 or '71, then another one on Spring Street. I was also on Greene Street, then on Washington Street—a carriage house—for ten years, then moved to Greenwich Street.

EWR: Why did you choose to stay in New York?

MH: I am a New York artist. I am not a Nevada artist.

EWR: What about New York holds such appeal?

MH: It is the center of the planet, and I'm certain it will be for years to come. People get optimistic that other areas will take it away. I have done shows in Los Angeles, but there is nothing comparable to New York. Los Angeles has its own art. I invested in both cities because I consider myself an American artist, not just a New York artist. I started to buy this land in Nevada in 1969 or '70. I would drive from here to Las Vegas, fly to New York, stay an indeterminate amount of time, then fly back to Las Vegas, come back here, then back again for years.

EWR: You have made work in all of these places, and sometimes multiple versions of the same sculpture. For example, *Rift* and *Dissipate*, which were part of the Nine Nevada Depressions, were originally made here in the desert and now exist permanently at the Menil Collection in Houston, Texas. How do you think of an artwork differently when the location changes?

MH: The first were the originals, pure dirt sculpture—and they weathered. I have photos on the dry lake showing *Rift* weathering, *Dissipate* dissipating on the Black Rock. The original works are gone. What exists today is made of steel. They are made at the exact same measurements, one foot wide and one foot deep. The works don't change, the places change, and the results vary.

EWR: Is it important that the measurements remain the same?

MH: After remaking the originals years ago, I could make any one of them at any size, but never have.

EWR: I ask the question because suburban Maryland is very different from southern Nevada. I am interested to hear your perspective on how the works will change when we install them at Glenstone.

MH: Like on Mars there is no oxygen, here there is oxygen. I don't think the aesthetics are any different. The surroundings change how integrated the artwork is with its environment. If you can build it inside, you might as well show it inside. If you can't build it inside, then you can't show it inside. That's the difference, portability. If it's fourteen hundred feet long and weighs eighty million tons, you aren't going to put it into the Metropolitan. Moving things from place to place alters the referential and environmental associations.

I've been liberating art from the gallery since 1968. I tried to do my first show at Dwan Gallery in the landfill where they were building the World Trade Towers. I have photos in it at about forty feet deep. Marion Javits—wife of Senator Jacob Javits—tried to help me persuade the city to let me install my first show there. But no one could help with the Port Authority. So, in 1969, I built *Double Negative* on Mormon Mesa in Nevada after giving up in Manhattan, since it wasn't going to happen there. I maintained the art—the standards didn't change, the place changed. The environment of art and the art itself are inseparable. The work is bonded to its place.

EWR: That's why it is so important for us to use the same type of surfaces, like the argillite we sourced for the works at Glenstone. Situating them in an open-air context also preserves a part of the original intent. When I first proposed that we take the roof off the pavilion for *Collapse*, I got a lot of blank stares, but it happened. But there is also the element of uncertainty that comes into focus when you take a piece outside into an uncontrolled environment. Have chance and contingency always been important to you?

MH: What I live by is chaos. Leaves will fall in it, birds will fall in it; then you'll clean it up—that's what you do. That's part of the cosmetics of materials. I'm not overly impressed by museum installations I have run across; they are totally insipid if you ask me. Don't you think there are enough buildings with roofs in the world? What is one building without a roof? There are a bunch of examples—places with smoke holes and sweat lodges, and there's the Pantheon in Rome. This is a tradition you are going to restart.

EWR: If you were to link your work to a historical tradition, would you link it to modernism or look more to prehistoric times?

MH: Posthistoric. I made a series of drawings, fifteen or twenty of them, made with oil, pastel, gouache, colored pencil, pencil, photo silk screens. Probably the best works of my life. They are titled the Post Historic series. In a moment I did a dozen really good ones. I had to stop everything to make them. Posthistoric means after the historic period; I think we are in a posthistoric period. I think the world went back to center in the '70s and '80s, where it reached a breaking point. I'm not the only one who thinks that. The oceans are about 90 percent dead, viruses are taking over, the water is poisoned, the ice is melting, everyone wants more bombs, there are too many humans, there is consensus that more species are becoming endangered—I'm seeing it here. I would say posthistoric is the theme. It is ominous, apocalyptic.

EWR: So even here you have that same feeling?

MH: Yes, I do, even living here. A lot of the things I say are out of Mark Twain humor and usually misinterpreted, but I think the world is in deep trouble.

EWR: If that is what is happening to our civilization, who do you make your art for?

MH: Myself. If I were making it for people I would be out of business. This isn't a business. I just really like doing it—a lot. I work hard to be able to do what I like to do. I don't think I have any big purpose in life.

EWR: Let's talk about stewardship. You have been working on *City* for more than forty years. It is a work of colossal proportions and extreme complexity. Do you spend time thinking about who will take care of it in the future?

MH: We spend time thinking about it, but this *City* project is big, and we don't have the answer yet. Will I spend my whole life building something to give to a caretaker? Or turn it into a visitor's center, like Abraham Lincoln's house in Illinois, with its small rooms, newspapers, and teacups scattered around? It's kind of corny, but they made it look like the Lincolns were still there. Stewardship? You got me. I'm not interested in that. I don't have big plans about the public, their entrée, or how many should come. I don't want to know about it.

EWR: But you want somebody to handle it.

MH: I know, but I can't seem to get into it; it's like trying to breathe underwater. You can't think about it. It doesn't make sense to turn the project into a circus for visitors.

EWR: But you don't think people coming to see the works we have at Glenstone would compromise them?

MH: You are the receptacle. It is done in an acknowledged way, and you know what the intent is. It's a museum, and it is supposed to be visited by people. I know the *City* will be seen by people, I just don't know the semantics of how it will happen.

EWR: You are putting a lot of trust in us. We certainly don't take that for granted and will make sure that the public will see the works the way you intend for them to be seen.

MH: I wouldn't have done this if I didn't have trust. Public art and all the things that happen when art is publicly produced are usually bad. I will not accept commissions anymore. I just read something Bob Morris said, that when the artwork gets bigger it implies public art. I disagree with that. I don't make it big because it's public art. I make it big because that's the way it should be.

EWR: You have mentioned places like Chichén Itzá as reference points for the scale of some of your biggest works.

MH: These places are inspirational to me. They impact me because of what I experienced there. I felt that is how sculpture should be. One of the definitions of sculpture that has become modernistically pursued is size. The Frederic Remingtons I have in my house remind me that sculptures can even sit on a table. But if you want to get to the power of sculpture, then you come to size. The Egyptians definitely did it at Abu Simbel and the Colossi of Memnon some forty-two hundred years ago. And some sculptors developed it in this country, but not from looking at earlier sculptures—only because the time had come for many reasons. I think it is now a constituent of American sculpture. I often remember the great Tony Smith. I met an Italian dealer years ago in Italy and he said the *Actual Size* projectors were too big, too American.

EWR: So that's when you knew you had it right.

MH: Exactly. Size is now a constant in the dialogue. Sculptures were once made for decorating cathedrals. Those days are over.

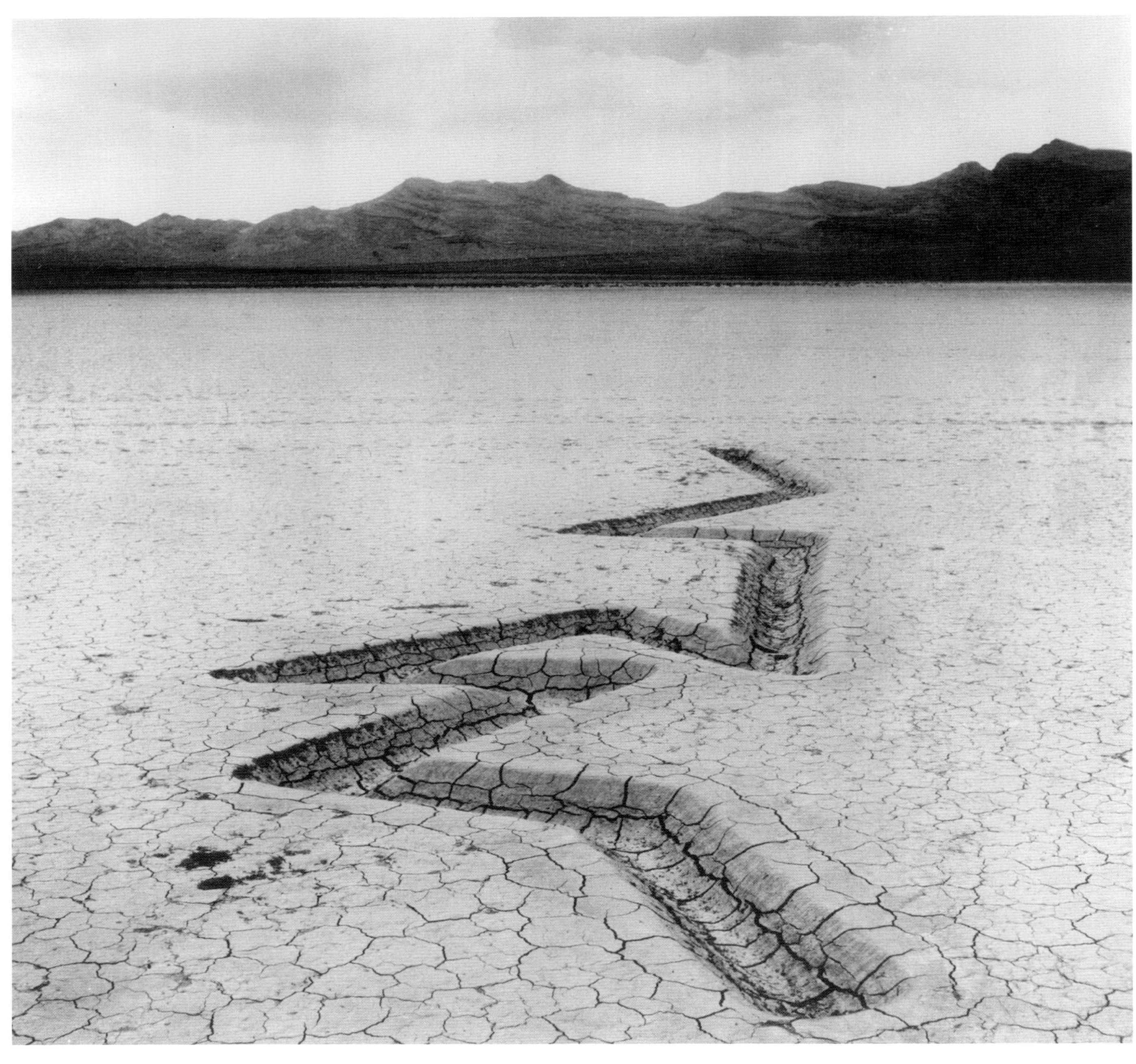

To create *Rift I*, 1968, the artist carved out one and a half tons of earth from Jean Dry Lake in Nevada. Over time, the piece deteriorated until it returned entirely to the flat desert from which it came.

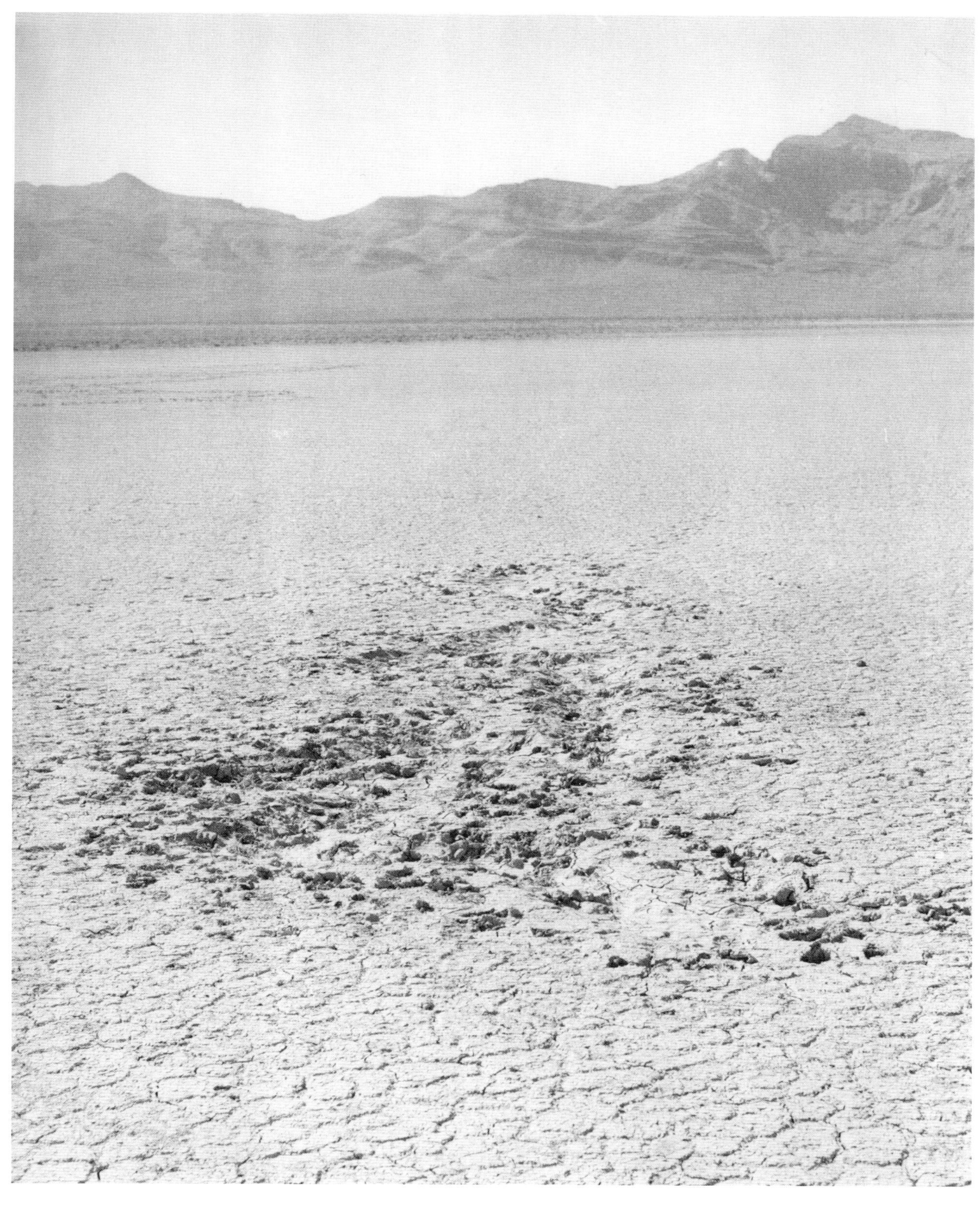

Rift I, one of the Nine Nevada Depressions, is pictured following the winter of 1968–1969, as it fades slowly back into the landscape at the end of its installation.

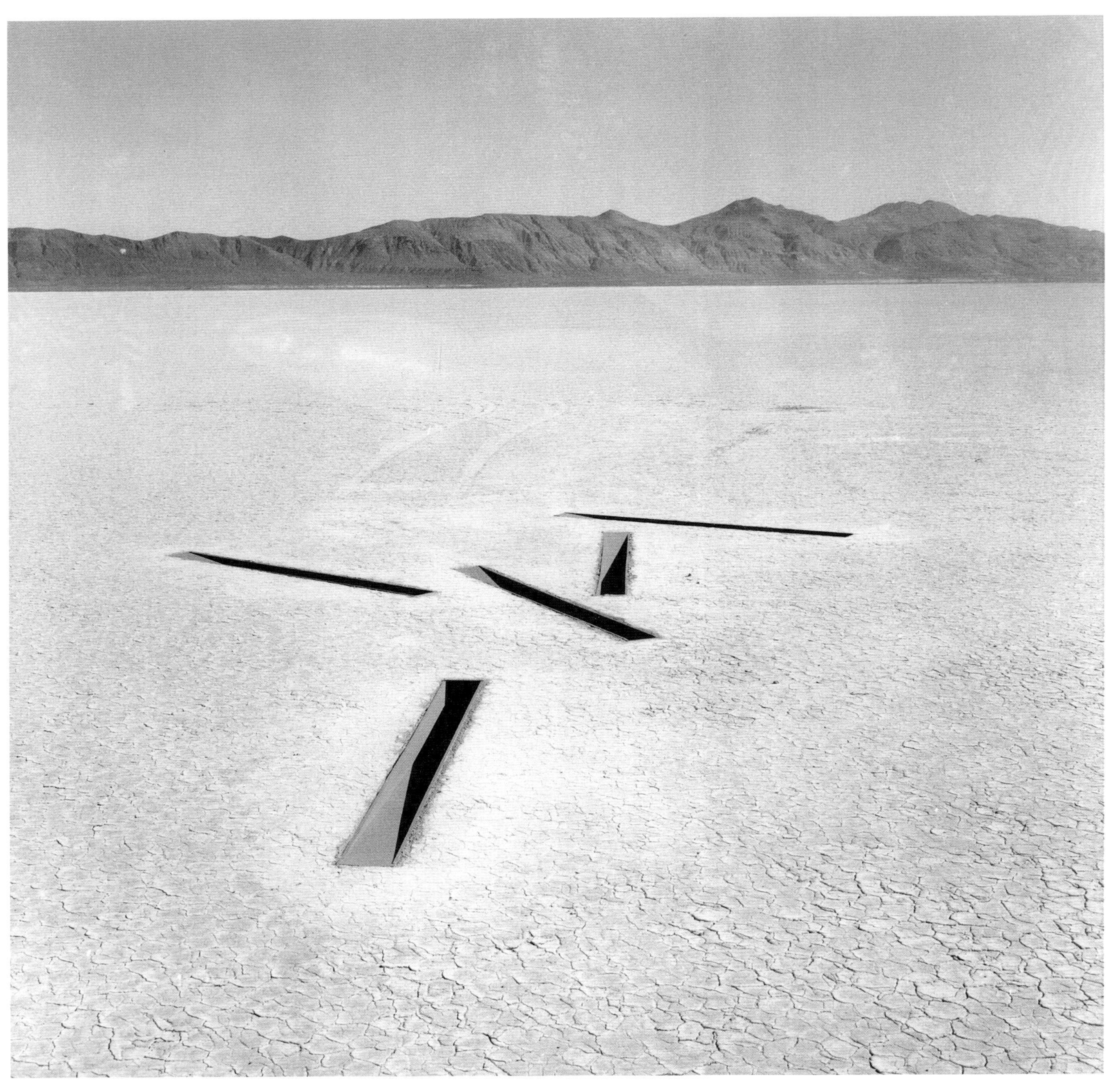

One of the Nine Nevada Depressions, *Dissipate*, 1968, was created by digging five trenches in the desert to make room for weathering-steel trays, which had variable depths.

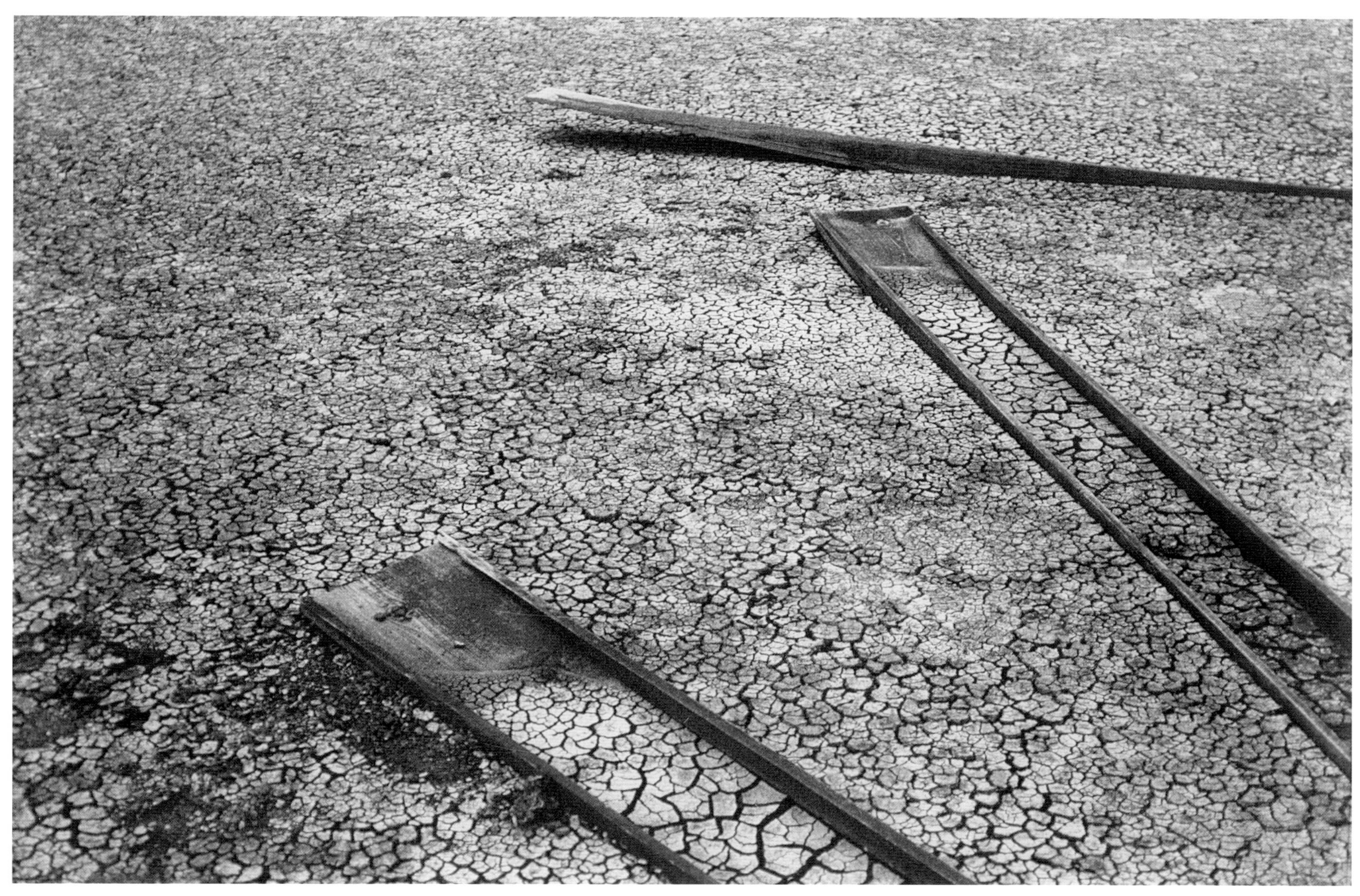

A detail of *Dissipate 2*, 1968, this image illustrates the wood tray elements that comprised the sculpture laid out in the Nevada desert. Conceived to deteriorate slowly back into the landscape, the sculpture's wood elements eventually cut deeper into the terrain, as shown above.

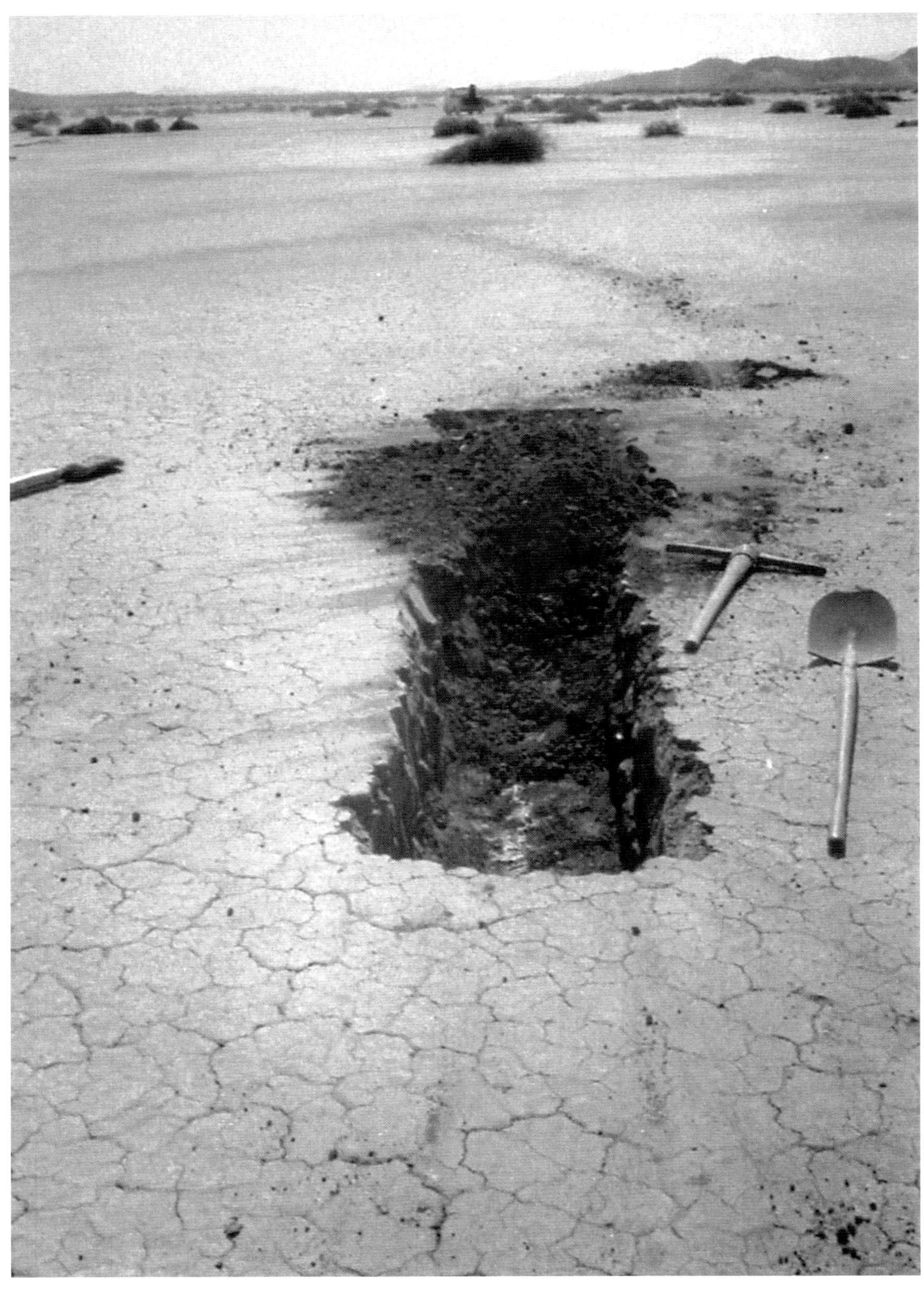

The beginning stages of excavation for the first *Compression Line*, realized by the artist in 1968 in El Mirage Dry Lake in the Mojave Desert in California. This inaugural effort measured sixteen feet long and was carved from wood.

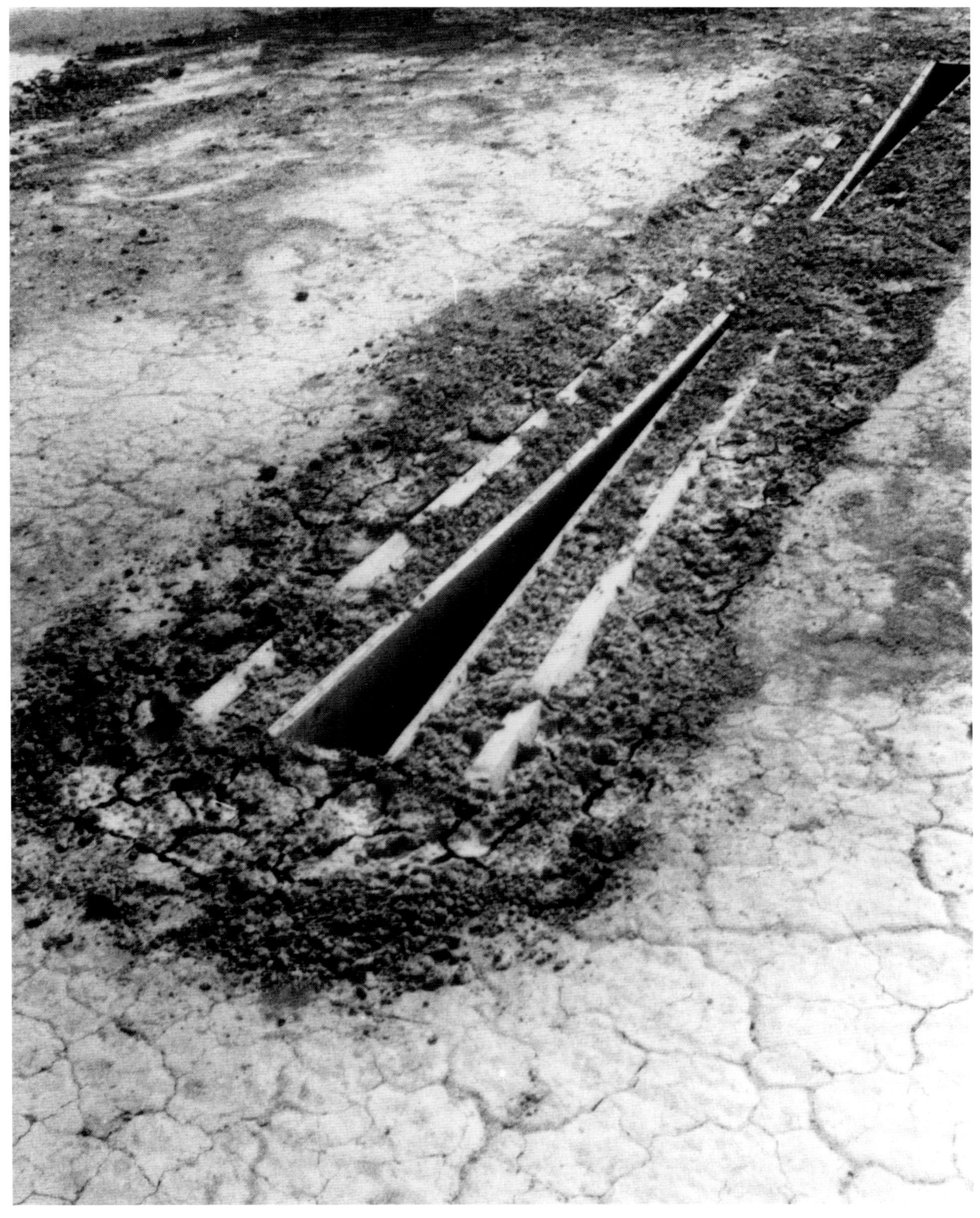

The predecessor to the work realized at Glenstone, *Compression Line*, 1968 (conceived to deteriorate back into the landscape) was created by placing a wood structure inside an excavated area of barren landscape. The same method the artist employed in 2016 was used to compact the side walls: slow, methodical compression of native soil until the center points of the parallel sides are forced to touch.

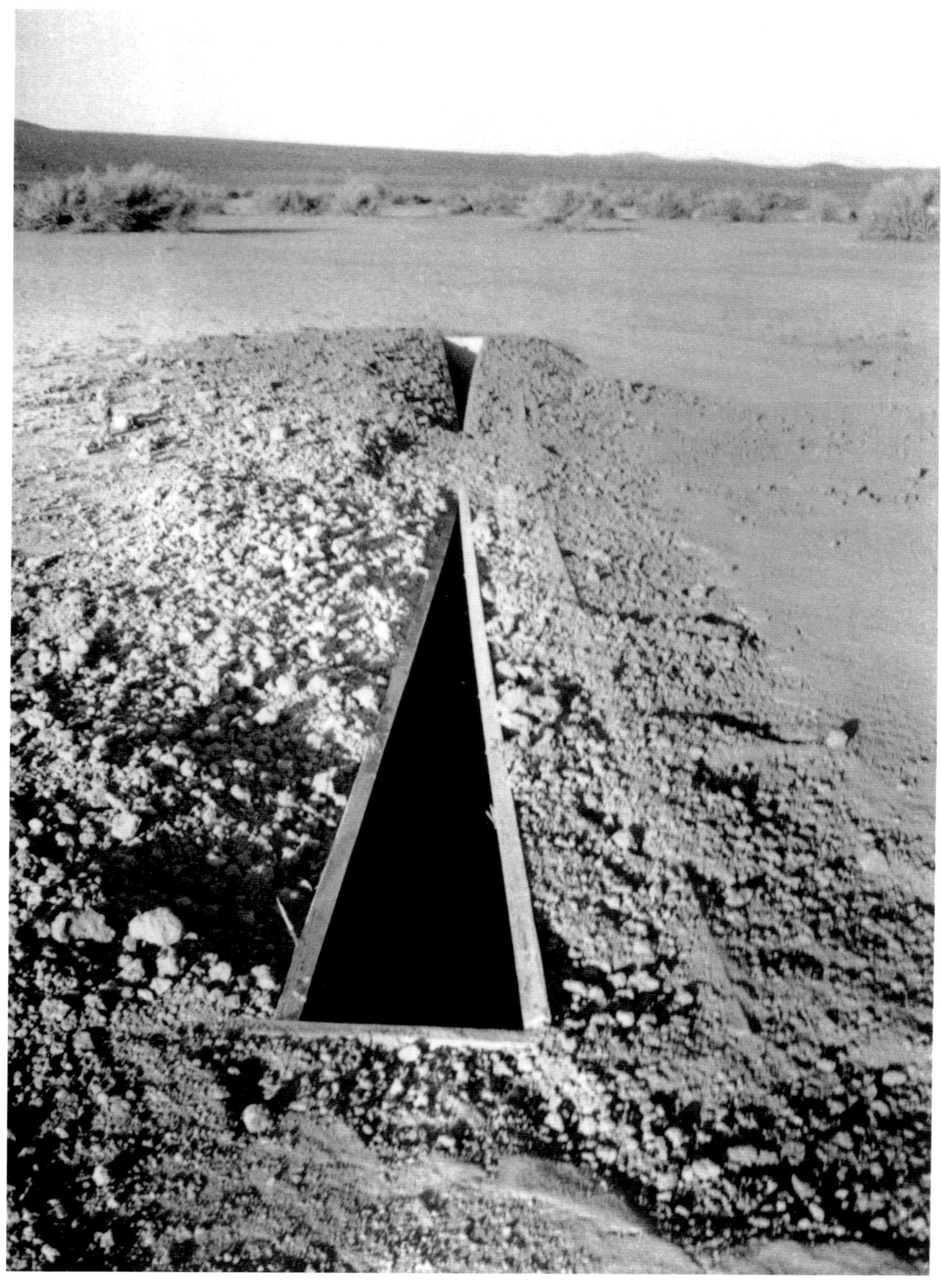

This image of the original *Compression Line* highlights the remarkable consistency of the artist's vision over the course of his career. Despite the differences in the very earth in which the sculptures are created, Glenstone's version is immediately recognizable as the manifestation of the concept developed by the artist decades ago.

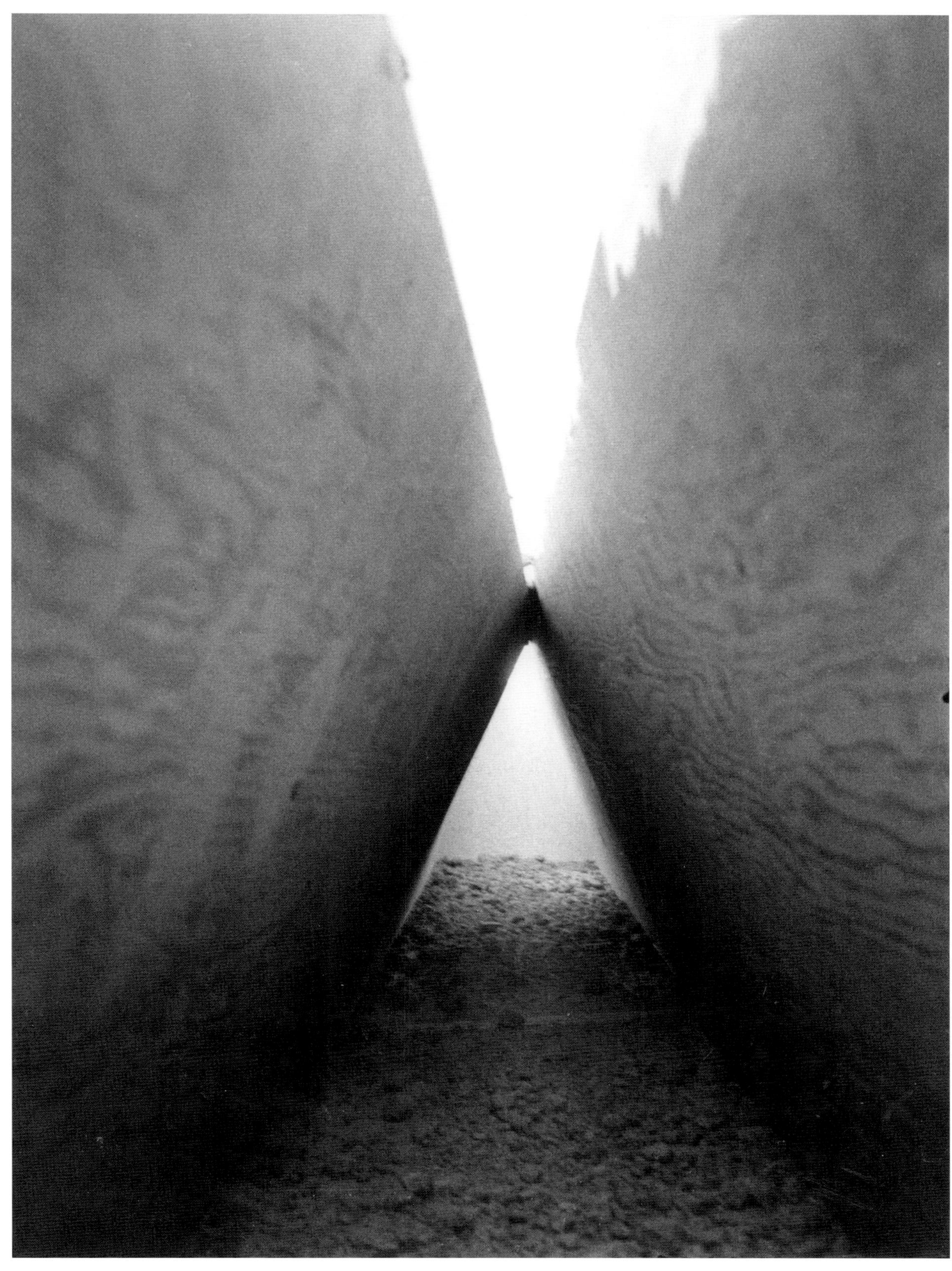

The interior of the sculpture reveals the volume of negative space conceived by the artist, and emphasizes the point where the parallel sides of the compression structure touch.

Afterword

This publication commemorates the opening of the Pavilions at Glenstone.

The building, designed by Thomas Phifer and Partners, was conceived as a series of eleven discrete pavilions surrounding a central water court. Contained within these pavilions are presentations of artwork, many devoted to single-artist installations. Seven of these special presentations are accompanied by monographic publications, of which this is one.

We see the Pavilions as the fullest realization to date of our mission to seamlessly integrate art, architecture, and landscape within a single, holistic visitor experience. It is the centerpiece of a fifteen-year campus-wide master-planning effort, led by landscape architects Peter Walker and Partners, which involved the reconfiguration and expansion of our public entrance, amenities, and walking trails. Throughout this process we have also deepened our commitment to organic, regenerative landscape practices, making Glenstone a leader in the field of sustainable environmental management.

With the opening of the Pavilions, we broaden access to Glenstone's grounds as well as its collection of postwar and contemporary art. Every time you visit, our attentive and well-informed guides will be available to answer questions and to hear you speak about *your* unique perspective on the Glenstone experience.

Admission to the museum and programs is, and will always be, free of charge.

We look forward to welcoming you.

Emily Wei Rales and Mitchell P. Rales
Founders
October 2018

Published on the occasion of the opening of the Pavilions at Glenstone in 2018.

Editors: Emily Wei Rales, Nora Severson Cafritz, Ali Nemerov
Editorial Assistant: Fanna Gebreyesus
Copy Editor: Claire Lehmann
Glenstone photography: Jerry Thompson, Paul Tukey
Design: Joseph Logan, Rachel Hudson, Katy Nelson
Printer: Meridian Printing
Published by: Glenstone Museum

First Edition:

Images courtesy:
Michael Heizer, p. 6, pp. 38–45

Glenstone Museum
12100 Glen Road
Potomac, Maryland 20854
www.glenstone.org

Printed and bound in the United States

Available through
ARTBOOK | D.A.P.
75 Broad Street, Suite 630
New York, NY 10004
www.artbook.com

ISBN: 978-0-9801086-7-5
LCCN: 2018948249